and

chasing
AMY

MIRAMAX
BOOKS

HYPERION
new york

CLeRKS

and

chasing AMY

two screenplays by

kevin smith

Library of Congress Cataloging-in-Publication Data

Smith, Kevin, 1970–
    Clerks and Chasing Amy : two screenplays / by Kevin Smith. — 1st
ed.
      p. cm.
    ISBN 0-7868-8263-8
    1. Motion picture plays.   I. Smith, Kevin, 1970–   Chasing Amy.
II. Title.   III. Title: Chasing Amy.
PN1997.A1S57   1997
791.43′75—dc21   96–40228
                                                CIP

Clerks production stills by Ed Hapstak
Chasing Amy still photographs by Lorenzo Bevilaqua and Monica Hampton
Bluntman & Chronic/*Chasing Amy* artwork by Mike Allred

Designed by Kathy Kikkert

First Edition

10 9 8 7 6 5 4 3 2 1

For Joey—who sat through many new ''theories'' and talked me though countless processing complications with wonderful patience, suffered me like a child, maintained her honor and dignity in the face of my insecure accusations, and continues to help me understand the simple lesson that comprehension of the past, not condemnation, is the only manner in which to neutralize insecurity . . . and all while still making *me* feel like the smart one.

contents

introduction: a "c" average

This is a story about a couple of journalists from what may be considered subversive newspapers, and how what they scribbled down in an effort to make a deadline changed my life. Twice.

I used to work in this convenience store.

Not a bad gig—long hours sometimes, but not very strenuous. To be quite honest, it was a lot like going to Vegas: You saw a lot of cash that wasn't yours, you could eat mountains of food for next to nothing, and the floor show was a mind-bending spectacle.

And to round out the metaphor, I hit the jackpot at said convenience store. I made a little picture about life in the slow lane, which seemed to go over well with some folks who'd either been there or wanted to view those collars of blue with anthropological curiosity and distance. It won some awards at a couple of high-profile film festivals (Sundance and Cannes), and lifted me out of obscurity, giving me not just international acclaim, but a better per-hour gig as well.

But I'm going to take you back for a second, to a time before the glory, before my parents' mantra became "Why do the characters have to curse so much?" and before my practice of jaded optimism would eventually pan out, careerwise.

One evening, I sat behind the register reading the world-renowned *Village Voice*. This was a time when New York City was still somewhat foreign and exotic to me. "New Yawk" was the dystopian landscape where those nasty orange license plates were handed out; the fantastical black market where you were supposedly able to buy *anything*—from switchblades and fake IDs, to Spanish fly and snuff films—right on the street; the shallow gene pool where the "Bennys" who swarmed our local beaches annually heralded from, filling the air with such colorful colloquialisms as, "If that fuckin' Frisbee even lands *near* my towel, I'm gonna shove it in your mother's ass like a fuckin' anal diaphragm, you fuckin' douchebag!" or, "Bobby just took a fuckin' shit in the rocks over de're!"

I'd always been a fan of movies (very important—not *film,* but movies), so I was pupil-deep in the cinema listings when I saw a photo of a guy, not that much older-looking than myself, being profiled in an article—the caption of which read, "Richard Linklater is the person that IFFM attendees most wanted to be." I read on—this chap Linklater had made a movie a year prior, and it was getting high marks from many folks, including the article's author—Amy Taubin. Ms. Taubin (Like that? I learned to do that from the *New York Times*) went on to describe indie film and this annual marketplace called the Independent Feature Film Market, where this guy Linklater was "the man," apparently. I removed the article from the paper and saved it, to remind myself to see the film.

If you follow me or my press, you know that Richard Linklater's *Slacker* is the film that made me decide to become a filmmaker (so thank or hate Richard). I saw it shortly after pulling that article from the *Voice,* and from the midnight screening I caught at the Angelika on, I knew what I wanted to be when I grew up.

The next morning, I got a frame and placed Amy Taubin's article in it, hanging it near my desk, beside my word processor. It inspired me.

I immersed myself in indie film (See? This is where *movies* become *films*), watching everything that had come before, everything that had come since my awakening. It was months before the irony struck me that New York—that oh-so-foreign terrain—had become a second home to me, what with all the after-work (read midnight) screenings my film compatriot Vincent and I would take in; as suburban as we were, nothing could keep us out of the Angelika's Friday or Saturday midnight shows (not even the eve/morn we emerged from the theater after seeing *Bad Lieutenant* only to find the car had been robbed, including the bag in which I'd been keeping all my notes on what was to be my first film, "In-Convenience").

When I'd finished *Clerks,* I knew I had to bring it to the IFFM, as per Ms. Taubin's article. For those not familiar with the setup, the entrant pays five hundred bucks for a screening slot. By means of self-promotion (read—bugging the shit out of people with jobs), the entrant cajoles, pleads, and threatens various industry-connected, badge-wearing gentry into coming to said screening, in hopes of securing that Holy Grail of every indie filmster: distribution.

Well, no one showed up at our screening. There were ten people in the audience—most of them cast and friends. But there was one guy, name of Bob Hawk, who sat waaaaaaaaaay up in the front of the theater, eyes glued on the screen. After the show, he told my producer/friend Scott that he was going to suggest the film to the Sundance Film Festival, amongst others. Since he wore a badge that marked no import (read—didn't say Miramax), we thought nothing of his claims.

Then, the next morning, I got a phone call.

"Is Kevin Smith there?"

"This is he."

"Kevin, this is Amy Taubin with the *Village Voice*."

Beat.

"Yeah, right. Who is this really?"

"Amy Taubin."

"Amy Taubin's calling my apartment. Okay. C'mon, Mom—this is you, isn't it?"

This went on for some time. Patient saint that she was, Ms. Taubin played along, until I was finally convinced it was she.

"Someone told me I should watch your film. I didn't get a chance to see it at the Market, but I'd like to take a look at it, and possibly include it in the Market wrap-up piece I'm doing."

"Why? Nobody showed up for it."

"People are talking about your film. They're calling it 'the undiscovered gem' of the Market."

That Bob Hawk. What a guy.

After trying to assimilate this heart-stopping news, I mustered up enough composure to share with Ms. Taubin the fact that I had the article she'd written about Richard framed, and hanging on my wall. She seemed somewhat dubious, then touched. I took down an address to send a tape to, and that was that.

Two weeks later, our phone-convo antics and *Clerks* became the centerpiece for Ms. Taubin's column on the IFFM. It was the first significant press we'd received, and contained one of the most accurate assessments of my work to date:

". . . it makes absence of style a virtue in its depiction of blue-collar depression and desire."

My style was that I had no style.

I felt validated as an independent filmmaker. But more important, I felt like I'd been welcomed into the club.

Cut to a couple years later. The flavor of the year (*Clerks* had tremendous staying power) had long lost its taste, and there I sat in my office, surrounded by bad reviews for my sophomore effort, *Mallrats*. Oh, sure—there were a handful of good ones from critics who got the joke, but on the whole, the reviews were savage.

Now, I'm no thin-skinned "artiste." I don't mind somebody not digging on what I do. Nothing is for everybody. But the critical reception to *'Rats* was just sad. Sad, because the movie (catch that?) wasn't really reviewed as much as *I* was for having the bad sense to make it (the tone was generally split between "He should know better" and "How dare he?"). I was a bit morose, because, even though I knew I had a beating coming to me (sophomore jinx—if they could bottle a way to beat it . . .) you always hope *everyone* will understand what you were trying to accomplish. Instead, I was roundly thrashed as the example of what happens when a neotalent gets some money to work with. Easy, easy criticism for the whipping boy of the moment.

And then my eyes fell on an obscure piece I hadn't really seen before.

The paper was the *NYPress,* and the author was a guy I'd never heard of—Matt Zoller Seitz. The review follows:

I didn't see Kevin Smith's *Clerks* in the theaters, so when I finally got around to watching it on video, my perceptions were loaded by reviews I'd read hyping it as a savage satire on the modern American workplace and a furious kiss-off to all those touchy-feely Gen-X comedies that have cluttered up multiplexes in the past few years.

But the film took me by surprise in a couple of ways. Look beyond the sexist, scatological dialogue, and *Clerks* is perversely sweet-natured and retro. It's basically a romantic comedy about a guy torn between two women, desperate to commit but afraid of the responsibility—kind of like a John Hughes movie, only dirtier. Viewed in that context, the script's foul-mouthed cynicism seems almost endearingly desperate—the defensive posturing of guys who fear and loathe women yet pine for true love.

The other surprise was how often Smith conjured up odd original images that were clearly personal, like when the hero calls his buddies together for an impromptu round of roller hockey on the roof of the convenience store that's crushing his spirit. A filmmaker doesn't include a scene like that to drive home a metaphor; he includes it because he really likes roller hockey.

Mallrats, Smith's studio-financed follow-up revisits the same basic terrain, but there are fewer personal touches. Filmed at the Mall of America, the titanic consumer fortress in suburban Minneapolis, the picture uses chatter about shopping-crazy America and satirical re-creations of mall culture (including stores called "Fashionable Male" and "Have a Cookie") to spin another story of two male buddies coping with gal trouble . . .

Smith writes wonderfully elaborate dialogue that couples the schoolboy erudition of Whit Stillman with free-floating obscenities and gross-out images. And his large cast of supporting characters is always fun to watch. Unfortunately, *Mallrats* is patchy, slow and annoyingly insincere in places, probably because Smith is paying homage to a genre (early-80s teen flicks) that wasn't very sincere to begin with. The film is further hampered by Smith's taste for very broad slapstick, which he clearly loves but doesn't really understand how to stage. Throughout the film, Jay and Silent Bob indulge in an escalating series of absurd confrontations with mall security and the game-show people; in one scene, Silent Bob sails through the air on a rope, then smashes through a dressing-room door where a woman is trying on clothes. Sure, the gag is faintly amusing, in the way that *Caddyshack* is faintly amusing when you're channel-surfing late at night. But I like the film better when it's quieter and subtler—when Smith's verbose, insecure characters yammer on endlessly about their love troubles, scam on the opposite sex and debate niggling aspects of mall culture.

Mallrats is almost worth seeing just for skateboarder [Jason] Lee's sublimely obnoxious performance as Brodie; he's so full of befuddled indignation at the world that he seems torn between barricading him-self in the Food Court with a rifle and withering away in weepy de-spair. The film's high point comes during his surprise appearance on the game show, where he stridently insists that "making whoopee" be referred to as "fucking," then launches into an apropos-of-nothing monologue about how passengers on an apparently doomed airplane flight began beating off furiously as they plunged to earth. Minutes later, he makes a gushy romantic declaration to Rene that wouldn't seem out of place in a Frank Capra picture, yet Lee's actorly gears shift so smoothly that you never doubt it for a second.

At moments like this, Smith's fog of thin satire, physical hijinks, and faux-jaded posturing dissipates, and you glimpse the filmmaker's ideal world: a fool's paradise where cynicism is redeemed by love, and love by cynicism. After seeing this movie I think I've figured out why the enigmatic Silent Bob doesn't like to talk: whenever he opens his mouth, everyone realizes what a sweet guy he is.

Now that just blew me away. Here was an assessment of my work that I hadn't seen in the mountains of negative yapping about my cinematic atrocity. And while it was by no means a positive review, this person had taken the time to *think about*—not *react to*—the movie. And in doing so, actually accomplished something that isn't necessarily the responsibility, nor ordinarily the aim of a film critic, but is more productive than a simple ''thumbs down'' or ''no stars'' can ever be.

It influenced me.

The closing comment in Mister Seitz's piece stuck with me. For everything my second effort had been deemed, nobody bothered to point out anything but the most superficial, the most obvious. It took a brother who actually gave the movie and his critique some consideration (instead of regurgitating knee-jerk bile all over the page) to help me gain insight into what exactly was happening with my work—on the top, around the corners . . . but especially deep inside.

I started writing *Chasing Amy* that day.

Months later, I feel it's the most honest and pure piece I've ever written.

I'd like to thank this pair of unsung heroes who—while basically doing their jobs—lifted me up, dusted me off, and helped put me on (and then back on) the path of both my profession and my life. Without their encouragement (whether intended or not), I'd have made it past neither the still-somewhat-stinging slamming I'd undergone . . . or the register of that store.

You know that thing they say about the pen?

All true.

I'd also like to take a second to thank some other folks. Scotty, who's sacrificed so much of his life to dwell in mine; my parents, who, though they haven't really ''gotten it'' until now, have always been supportive of my job; Harvey and the good folks at Miramax, who've stepped up to the plate for both of these flicks; Brian, Jeff, Ben, Joey, Jason Lee, Dwight, Jason Mewes, and the entire casts and crews of both *Clerks* and *Amy,* who've made both films theirs as much as mine; Bob Hawk and John Pierson, who've been there from the start, and I hope will be there at the end; Kristin and the folks at Hyperion who bit their tongues every time I wanted to add something to the book; and anyone who's ever sat down to watch either flick, whether in the theater or on video—I hope I've at least made you laugh or made you think.

Or both.

Kevin Smith
January 15, 1996

INT: BEDROOM. EARLY-MORNING HOURS

A DOG *sleeps on a neatly made bed.*
A CLOCK *reads twenty to six.*
A SHELF OF BOOKS *holds such classics as* Dante's Inferno, Beyond
Good and Evil, The Catcher in the Rye, *and* The Dark Knight Returns. A
FRAMED DIPLOMA, *dusty and unkempt, hangs askew on the wall. A
snapshot of a girl is stuck in the corner, and a bra weighs one end down.*
A PHONE *sits quietly atop a bundle of laundry. It suddenly explodes with
a resounding ring—once, twice, three times.* A CLOSET DOOR *swings
open, and a half-clad figure falls out.* THE PHONE *rings yet again, and
a hand falls upon the receiver, yanking it off the trash can, OC.* THE
RUMPLED FIGURE *lays with his back to the camera, phone in hand.*

> FIGURE
> *(groggily)*
> Hello . . . What? . . . No, I don't work today. . . . I'm playing
> hockey at two.

THE DOG *yawns and shakes its head.*

> FIGURE (OC)
> Why don't you call Randal? . . . Because I'm fucking tired. . . . I
> just closed last night. . . .
> *(deep sigh)*
> Jesus . . . What time are you going to come in? . . . Twelve . . . Be
> there by twelve? . . . Swear . . .

A PICTURE OF A GIRL *leans against a trophy. The picture is decorated
with a Play-Doh beard and mustache.*

FIGURE (OC)
Swear you'll be in by twelve and I'll do it. . . .
Twelve . . . Twelve or I walk.

THE PHONE RECEIVER *slams into the cradle.* THE RUMPLED
FIGURE *slowly sits up and remains motionless. He musses his hair and
stands.*
THE DOG *stands and wags its tail. A hand pats its head. The Rumpled
Figure lays down on the bed. We now see his face. It is the face of* DANTE
and this is Dante's room; this is Dante's life. DANTE *grabs the dog and
wrestles it.*

                              DANTE
          Next time, I get the bed.

He releases the dog and sits up.

                              DANTE
                           (exhausted)
          Shit.

Cut to:

INT: BATHROOM. MINUTES LATER

*A steaming shower fills the room. The dog licks water from the toilet. Cut
to:*

INT: KITCHEN. MINUTES LATER

A towel-dressed DANTE *opens the fridge and peers inside. He grabs a
half-empty gallon of milk and closes the door. Cut to:*

INT: KITCHEN. SECONDS LATER

*Chocolate milk mix is heaped into a tumbler. One scoop, two scoops, three
scoops, four scoops. Cut to:*

INT: BEDROOM. A MINUTE LATER

DANTE *gulps his breakfast while feeling inside the closet for some
clothes. Some chocolate milk spills on the floor.* THE DOG *laps at the
small puddle of chocolate milk. Cut to:*

INT: HALLWAY. MINUTES LATER

DANTE'S *feet are hastily covered. A hand grabs keys from atop a VCR. Cut to:*

EXT: DRIVEWAY. MINUTES LATER

A car backs out of the driveway and speeds down the street. Cut to:

EXT: CONVENIENCE STORE. MORNING

The car pulls up, with a screech. Feet descend to the ground from the open door. Keys jam into a lock and pop it open. Cut to:

DANTE *lifts the metal shutter revealing the door. He opens it and grabs two bundles of papers, throwing them inside the store. Cut to:*

INT: CONVENIENCE STORE. MORNING

A very dark room barely lit by the daylight. Suddenly, the lights flick on, revealing the glorious interior of the convenience store. THE CAT *looks at* DANTE *as he passes the camera quickly.* THE PAPER BUNDLE *is snapped open with a knife. Newspapers slam into the appropriate racks. One rack remains empty. A coffee filter is placed in a metal pot. Ground coffee follows, and the mix is shoved into place in the coffeemaker. The switch is flicked and the machine comes to life. The empty newspaper rack with the heading* ASBURY PARK PRESS *seems out of place among all the other stacks of papers.* DANTE *rubs his chin and stares, puzzled. He rolls his eyes as it occurs to him.*

> DANTE
>
> Shit.

The register pops open, and a hand extracts a quarter. Cut to:

EXT: CONVENIENCE STORE. MORNING

POV: NEWSPAPER MACHINE

Through murky glass and thin metal grating, we see DANTE *approach. He stops and drops a quarter in the slot. He pulls the door down, finally allowing us a clear view as he reaches toward the camera.*

DANTE *pulls a stack of newspapers from the* Asbury Park Press *vending machine. He struggles to hold them all in one hand as he lets the door slam shut. He turns to walk away, but the sound of the quarter dropping into the change slot stops him. He takes a step back to grab the coin. Cut to:*

INT: CONVENIENCE STORE. MORNING

The papers drop into the once-empty rack with a resounding flop. The quarter drops back into the register drawer. Cut to:

EXT: CONVENIENCE STORE. MORNING

DANTE *tries to jam the key into the window shutter lock. He looks down at it.*

                              DANTE
          Shit!

The lock is gummed up with gum or something hard and obtrusive like gum, preventing the key from being inserted. DANTE *looks around and kicks the shutter angrily. The car trunk pops open and a hand reaches inside, pulling out a folded white sheet. Cut to:*

INT: CONVENIENCE STORE. MORNING

A can of shoe polish is grabbed from the shelf. DANTE *dips his fingers into the shoe polish and writes large letters on the unfurled sheet, leaning on the cooler. Cut to:*

EXT: CONVENIENCE STORE. MORNING

DANTE *stands on a garbage can and tucks a corner of the sheet under the awning. He jumps down. The banner reads* I ASSURE YOU, WE'RE OPEN. *The door sign shifts from* CLOSED *to* OPEN. *Cut to:*

INT: CONVENIENCE STORE. MORNING

The clock reads 6:20. DANTE *leans behind the counter, the morning routine completed. He stares ahead, catatonic, then drops his head in his hands. The day has begun. Cut to:*

EXT: CONVENIENCE STORE. DAY

The store, with its makeshift banner looming in the dim morning hour, just after dawn. A car drives by. Cut to:

INT: CONVENIENCE STORE. DAY

DANTE *waits on a customer* (ACTIVIST) *buying coffee.*

> DANTE
> Thanks. Have a good one.

> ACTIVIST
> Do you mind if I drink this here?

> DANTE
> Sure. Go ahead.

The ACTIVIST *leans on a briefcase and drinks his coffee. Another* CUSTOMER *leans in the door.*

> CUSTOMER
> Are you open?

> DANTE
> Yeah.

> CUSTOMER
> Pack of cigarettes.

> ACTIVIST
> Are you sure?

> CUSTOMER
> Am I sure?

> ACTIVIST
> Are you sure?

> CUSTOMER
> Am I sure about what?

> ACTIVIST
> Do you really want to buy those cigarettes?

CUSTOMER

Are you serious?

ACTIVIST

How long have you been smoking?

CUSTOMER
(to DANTE)

What is this, a poll?

DANTE

Beats me.

ACTIVIST

How long have you been a smoker?

CUSTOMER

Since I was thirteen.

The ACTIVIST *lifts his briefcase onto the counter. He opens it and extracts a sickly-looking lung model.*

ACTIVIST

I'd say you're about nineteen, twenty, am I right?

CUSTOMER

What in the hell is that?

ACTIVIST

That's your lung. By this time, your lung looks like this.

CUSTOMER

You're shittin' me.

ACTIVIST

You think I'm shitting you . . .

The ACTIVIST *hands him something from the briefcase.*

CUSTOMER

What's this?

ACTIVIST

It's a trach ring. It's what they install in your throat when throat cancer takes your voice box. This one came out of a sixty-year-old man.

CUSTOMER
(drops ring)

Unnhh!

ACTIVIST
(picks up the ring)

He smoked until the day he died. Used to put the cigarette in this thing and smoke it that way.

DANTE

Excuse me, but . . .

ACTIVIST

This is where you're heading. A cruddy lung, smoking through a hole in your throat. Do you really want that?

CUSTOMER

Well, if it's already too late . . .

ACTIVIST

It's never too late. Give those cigarettes back now, and buy some gum instead.
(grabs nearby pack, reads)
Here. Chewlies Gum. Try this.

CUSTOMER

It's not the same.

ACTIVIST

It's cheaper than cigarettes. And it certainly beats this.

Hands him a picture.

CUSTOMER

Jesus!

ACTIVIST

It's a picture of a cancer-ridden lung. Keep it.

CUSTOMER
(to DANTE)

I'll just take the gum.

DANTE

Fifty-five.

ACTIVIST

You've made a wise choice. Keep up the good work.

The CUSTOMER *exits.*

DANTE

Maybe you should take that coffee outside.

ACTIVIST

No, I think I'll drink it in here, thanks.

DANTE

If you're going to drink it in here, I'd appreciate it if you'd not bother the customers.

ACTIVIST

Okay. I'm sorry about that.

Another CUSTOMER *comes up to the counter.*

CUSTOMER

Pack of cigarettes.
> *(looks at model)*

What's that?

ACTIVIST

This? How long have you been smoking?

Cut to:

EXT: CONVENIENCE STORE. DAY

A blank wall. JAY *steps into the frame, followed by* SILENT BOB. JAY
pulls off his coat and swings it into the arms of SILENT BOB. JAY *then
throws down with a makeshift slam dance, spinning his arm and fake-
hitting* SILENT BOB.

JAY

WE NEED SOME TITS AND ASS! YEAH!

SILENT BOB *lights a smoke.*

JAY

I feel good today, Silent Bob. We're gonna make some money!
And then you know what we're going to do? We're going to go
to that party and get some pussy! I'm gonna fuck this bitch, that
bitch . . .
> (Blue Velvet *Hopper)*

I'LL FUCK ANYTHING THAT MOVES!

SILENT BOB *points to something off-screen.*

JAY
> *(to OC)*

What you looking at?! I'll kick your fucking ass!
> *(to* SILENT BOB*)*

Doesn't that motherfucker still owe me ten bucks?

SILENT BOB *nods.*

JAY

Tonight, you and me are going to rip off that fucker's head, and
take out his fucking soul! Remind me if he tries to buy something

from us, to cut it with leafs and twigs . . . or fucking shit in the motherfucker's bag!

Some girls walk past. JAY *smiles at them.*

JAY

Wa sup sluts?
(to SILENT BOB)
Damn Silent Bob! You one rude motherfucker! But you're cute as hell.
(slowly drops to knees)
I wanna go down on you, and suckle you.
(makes blow job neck-jerks)
And then, I wanna line up three more guys, and make like a circus seal . . .
JAY makes blow job faces down an imaginary line of guys, looking quite like a performing seal. He throws a little humming sound behind each nod. He then hops up quickly.

JAY

Ewwww! You fucking faggot! I fucking hate guys!
(yelling)
I LOVE WOMEN!
(calmer)
Neh.

A GUY comes up to them.

GUY

You selling?

JAY
(all business)
I got hits, hash, weed, and later on I'll have 'shrooms. We take cash, or stolen MasterCard and Visa.

Cut to:

INT: CONVENIENCE STORE. DAY

A SMALL CROWD gathers around the ACTIVIST as he orates. It has become something of a rally.

ACTIVIST
You're spending what? Twenty, thirty dollars a week on cigarettes.

LISTENER 1

Forty.

LISTENER 2

Fifty-three.

ACTIVIST

Fifty-three dollars. Would you pay someone that much money
every week to kill you? Because that's what you're doing now,
by paying for the so-called privilege to smoke!

LISTENER 3

We all gotta go sometime . . .

ACTIVIST

It's that kind of mentality that allows this cancer-producing
industry to thrive. Of course we're all going to die someday, but
do we have to pay for it? Do we have to actually throw hard-
earned dollars on a counter and say, ''Please, please, Mister
Merchant of Death, sir; please sell me something that will give
me bad breath, stink up my clothes, and fry my lungs.''

LISTENER 1

It's not that easy to quit.

ACTIVIST

Of course it's not; not when you have people like this mindless
cretin so happy and willing to sell you nails for your coffin!

DANTE

Hey, now wait a sec . . .

ACTIVIST

Now he's going to launch into his rap about how he's just doing his job; following orders. Friends, let me tell you about another bunch of hate mongers that were just following orders: they were called Nazis, and they practically wiped a nation of people from the Earth . . . just like cigarettes are doing now! Cigarette smoking is the new Holocaust, and those that partake in the practice of smoking or sell the wares that promote it are the Nazis of the nineties! He doesn't care how many people die from it! He smiles as you pay for your cancer sticks and says, "Have a nice day."

DANTE

I think you'd better leave now.

ACTIVIST

You want me to leave? Why? Because somebody is telling it like it is? Somebody's giving these fine people a wake-up call?!

DANTE

You're loitering in here, and causing a disturbance.

ACTIVIST

You're the disturbance, pal! And here . . . *(slaps a dollar on the counter)* I'm buying some . . . what's this? . . . Chewlie's Gum. There. I'm no longer loitering. I'm a customer, a customer engaged in a discussion with other customers.

LISTENER 2
(to DANTE)
Yeah, now shut up so he can speak!

ACTIVIST

Oh, he's scared now! He sees the threat we present! He smells the changes coming, and the loss of sales when the nonsmokers finally demand satisfaction. We demand the right to breathe cleaner air!

LISTENER 3

Yeah!

ACTIVIST

We'd rather chew our gum than embrace slow death! Let's abolish this heinous practice of sucking poison, and if it means ruffling the feathers of a convenience store idiot, then so be it!

DANTE

That's it, everybody out.

ACTIVIST

We're not moving! We have a right, a constitutional right, to assemble and be heard!

DANTE

Yeah, but not in here.

ACTIVIST

What better place than this? To stamp it out, you gotta start at the source!

DANTE

Like I'm responsible for all the smokers!

ACTIVIST

The ones in this town, yes! You encourage their growth, their habit. You're the source in this area, and we're going to shut you down for good! For good, cancer-merchant!

The small crowd begins to chant and jeer in DANTE's *face.*

CROWD

Cancer merchant! Cancer merchant! Cancer merchant!

VERONICA *enters and surveys the mess. The* CROWD *throws cigarettes at* DANTE, *pelting him in the face. Suddenly, a loud blast is heard, and white powder explodes over the throng. Everyone turns to face . . .*

VERONICA *as she stands on one of the freezer cases, holding a fire extinguisher.*

VERONICA

Who's leading this mob?

The CROWD *looks among themselves. Someone points to OC.*

SOMEONE

That guy.

The ACTIVIST *carries his briefcase surreptitiously toward the door.*

                    (OC) VERONICA

        Freeze.

VERONICA *jumps off the freezer case, training the nozzle of the*
extinguisher on the ACTIVIST.

                    VERONICA
        Let's see some credentials.

He reaches into his briefcase. She pokes the extinguisher nozzle at him,
warningly.

        Slowly . . .

He pulls out a business card and hands it to her. She reads it.

        You're a Chewlie's Gum representative?

He nods.

        And you're stirring up all this antismoking sentiment to . . . what?
        . . . sell more gum?

He nods again.

                    (through gritted teeth)

        Get out of here.

He quickly flees. She blasts him with more chemical as he exits.

                    (to the crowd)

        And you people: Don't you have jobs to go to?
        Get out of here and go commute.

The CROWD *sheepishly exits, one by one, offering apologetic glances.*
DANTE *tries to regain his composure.* VERONICA *watches the crowd*
disperse, disgusted.

        You oughta be ashamed of yourselves. Easily led automatons. Try
        thinking for yourselves before you pelt an innocent man with
        cigarettes.

The last of the crowd exits. VERONICA *sets the fire extinguisher down next to* DANTE. DANTE *is sitting on the floor, head in his folded arms.*

It looked like Tiananmen Square in here for a second.

DANTE is silent.

''Thank you, Veronica; you saved me from an extremely ugly mob scene.''

DANTE *remains silent.*

(sits beside him)

Okay, champ. What's wrong?

DANTE *lifts his head and shoots her a disgusted look.*

All right, stupid question. But don't you think you're taking this a bit too hard?

DANTE
Too hard?! I don't have enough indignities in my life—people start throwing cigarettes at me!

VERONICA
At least they weren't lit.

DANTE
I hate this fucking place.

VERONICA
Then quit. You should be going to school anyway . . .

DANTE
Please, Veronica. Last thing I need is a lecture at this point.

VERONICA
All I'm saying is that if you're unhappy you should leave.

DANTE
I'm not even supposed to be here today!

VERONICA

I know. I stopped by your house and your mom said you left at like six or something.

DANTE

The guy got sick and couldn't come in.

VERONICA

Don't you have a hockey game at two?

DANTE

Yes! And I'm going to play like shit because I didn't get a good night's sleep!

VERONICA

Why did you agree to come in then?

DANTE

I'm only here until twelve, then I'm gone. The boss is coming in.

VERONICA

Why don't you open the shutters and get some sunlight in here?

DANTE

Somebody jammed the locks with gum.

VERONICA

You're kidding.

DANTE

Bunch of savages in this town.

VERONICA

You look bushed. What time did you get to bed?

DANTE

I don't know—like two-thirty, three.

VERONICA

What were you doing up so late?

DANTE
(skirting)

Hunhh? Nothing.

                    VERONICA
                    (persistent)
What were you doing?

                    DANTE
Nothing! Jesus! I gotta fight with you now?

                    VERONICA
Who's fighting? Why are you so defensive?

                    DANTE
Who's defensive? Just . . . Would you just hug me?! All right?
Your boyfriend was accosted by an angry mob, and he needs to
be hugged.

She stares at him.

                    DANTE
What? What is that?

                    VERONICA
She called you, didn't she?

                    DANTE
Oh, be real! Would you . . . Would you please hug me? I just went
through a very traumatic experience and I haven't been having
the best day so far. Now come on.

VERONICA *stares at him.*

                    DANTE
What? What's with that look?! I wasn't talking to anyone,
especially her! Look at you, being all sort of . . . I don't know . . .
stand-offish.

VERONICA *looks away.*

                    DANTE
Fine. You don't trust me, don't hug me. I see how it is. All right
Pissy-pants, you just go on being suspicious and quiet. I don't
even want to hug you at this point.

VERONICA *looks back at him.*

DANTE

(pleadingly)

Give you a dollar?

Cut to:

INT: CONVENIENCE STORE. DAY

A NOTE *on the counter next to a small pile of money reads:*

PLEASE LEAVE MONEY ON THE COUNTER. TAKE CHANGE WHEN
APPLICABLE. BE HONEST.

DANTE *and* VERONICA *are slumped on the floor, behind the counter.*
VERONICA *holds* DANTE *in her arms, his head on her chest. Change is
heard hitting the counter.*

DANTE

(to OC customer)

Thanks.

The door is heard opening and closing—a customer leaving.

VERONICA

How much money did you leave up there?

DANTE

Like three dollars in mixed change and a couple of singles. People
only get the paper or coffee this time of morning.

VERONICA

You're trusting.

DANTE

Why do you say that?

VERONICA

How do you know they're taking the right amount of change? Or
even paying for what they take?

DANTE

Theoretically, people see money on the counter and nobody
around, they think they're being watched.

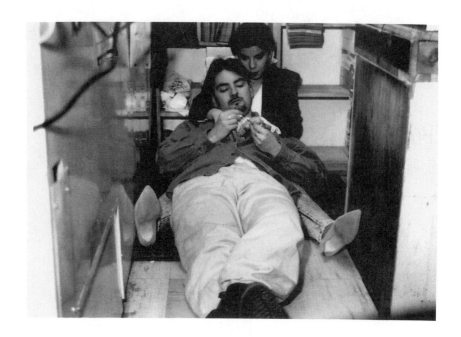

VERONICA

Honesty through paranoia. Why do you smell like shoe polish?

DANTE

I had to use shoe polish to make that sign. The smell won't come
off.

VERONICA

Do you think anyone can see us down here?

DANTE

Why? You wanna have sex or something?

VERONICA
(sarcastic)

Ooh! Can we?!

DANTE

Really?

VERONICA

I was kidding.

DANTE

Yeah, right. You can't get enough of me.

VERONICA

Typically male point of view.

DANTE

How do you figure?

VERONICA

You show some bedroom proficiency, and you think you're gods.
What about what we do for you?

DANTE

Women? Women, as lovers, are all basically the same: they just
have to be there.

VERONICA

''Be there?''

DANTE

Making a male climax is not all that challenging: insert
somewhere close and preferably moist; thrust; repeat.

VERONICA

How flattering.

DANTE

Now, making a woman cum . . . therein lies a challenge.

VERONICA

Oh, you think so?

DANTE

A girl makes a guy cum, it's standard. A guy makes a girl cum,
it's talent.

VERONICA

And I actually date you?

DANTE

Something wrong?

VERONICA

I'm insulted. Believe me, Don Juan, it takes more than that to get
a guy off. Just ''being there''—as you put it—is not enough.

DANTE
I touched a nerve.

VERONICA
I'm astonished to hear you trivialize my role in our sex life.

DANTE
It wasn't directed at you. I was making a broad generalization.

VERONICA
You were making a generalization about ''broads''!

DANTE
These are my opinions based on my experiences with the few women who were good enough to sleep with me.

VERONICA
How many?

DANTE
How many what?

VERONICA
How many girls have you slept with?

DANTE
How many different girls? Didn't we already have this discussion once?

VERONICA
We might have; I don't remember. How many?

DANTE
Including you?

VERONICA
It better be up to and including me.

DANTE
(pause to count)
Twelve.

VERONICA
You've slept with twelve different girls?

DANTE

Including you; yes.

Pause. She slaps him.

DANTE

What the hell was that for?

VERONICA

You're a pig.

DANTE

Why'd you hit me?

VERONICA

Do you know how many different men I've had sex with?

DANTE

Do I get to hit you after you tell me?

VERONICA

Three.

DANTE

Three?

VERONICA

Three including you.

DANTE

You've only had sex with three different people?

VERONICA

I'm not the pig you are.

DANTE

Who?

VERONICA

You!

DANTE

No; who were the three, besides me?

VERONICA

John Franson and Rob Stanslyk.

DANTE

(with true admiration)

Wow. That's great. That's something to be proud of.

VERONICA

I am. And that's why you should feel like a pig. You men make me sick. You'll sleep with anything that says yes.

DANTE

Animal, vegetable, or mineral.

VERONICA

Vegetable meaning paraplegic.

DANTE

They put up the least amount of struggle.

VERONICA

After dropping a bombshell like that, you owe me. Big.

DANTE

All right. Name it.

VERONICA

I want you to come with me on Monday.

DANTE

Where?

VERONICA

To school. There's a seminar about getting back into a scholastic program after a lapse in enrollment.

DANTE

Can't we ever have a discussion without that coming up?

VERONICA

It's important to me, Dante. You have so much potential that just goes to waste in this pit. I wish you'd go back to school.

DANTE

Jesus, would you stop? You make my head hurt when you talk about this.

VERONICA *stands, letting* DANTE'S *head hit the floor.*

DANTE

Shit! Why are we getting up?

VERONICA

Unlike you, I have a class in forty-five minutes.

A handsome young man (WILLAM) *is standing at the counter.*
VERONICA *reacts to him.*

VERONICA
(surprised)

Willam!

WILLAM

Ronnie! How are you? You work here now?

VERONICA
(locks arms with DANTE*)*

No, I'm just visiting my man.
(to DANTE*)*
Dante, this is Willam Black.
(to WILLAM*)*
This is Dante Hicks, my boyfriend.

DANTE

How are you? Just the soda?

WILLAM

And a pack of cigarettes.
(to VERONICA; *paying)*
Are you still going to Seton Hall?

VERONICA

No, I transferred into Monmouth this year. I was tired of missing him.
(squeezes DANTE'S *arm)*

WILLAM

Do you still talk to Sylvan?

VERONICA

I just talked to her on Monday. We still hang out on weekends.

WILLAM
(leaving)
That's cool. Well—you two lovebirds take it easy, all right?

VERONICA

I will. Take it easy.

WILLAM

Bye.

(exits)

VERONICA

Bye.
(to Dante)
That was Snowball.

DANTE

Why do you call him that?

VERONICA

Sylvan made it up. It's a blow job thing.

DANTE

What do you mean?

VERONICA

After he gets a blow job, he likes to have the cum spit back into his mouth while kissing. It's called snowballing.

DANTE

He requested this?

VERONICA

He gets off on it.

DANTE

Sylvan can be talked into anything.

VERONICA

Why do you say that?

DANTE

Like you said—she snowballed him.

VERONICA

Sylvan? No; I snowballed him.

DANTE

Yeah, right.

VERONICA

I'm serious. . . .

A moment of silence as DANTE'S *chuckles fade to comprehension.*

DANTE

You sucked that guy's dick?

VERONICA

Yeah. How do you think I knew he liked . . .

DANTE
(panicky)
But . . . but you said you only had sex with three
guys! You never mentioned him!

VERONICA

That's because I never had sex with him!

DANTE

You sucked his dick!

VERONICA

We went out a few times. We didn't have sex, but we fooled
around.

DANTE
(massive panic attack)
Oh my God! Why did you tell me you only slept with three guys?

VERONICA

Because I did only sleep with three guys! That doesn't mean I didn't just go with people.

DANTE

Oh my God—I feel so nauseous . . .

VERONICA

I'm sorry, Dante. I thought you understood.

DANTE

I did understand! I understood that you slept with three different guys, and that's all you said.

VERONICA

Please calm down.

DANTE

How many?

VERONICA

Dante . . .

DANTE

How many dicks have you sucked?!

VERONICA

Let it go . . .

DANTE

HOW MANY?

VERONICA

All right! Shut up a second and I'll tell you! Jesus! I didn't freak like this when you told me how many girls you fucked.

DANTE

This is different. This is important. How many?!

She counts silently, using fingers as marks. DANTE waits on a customer in the interim. VERONICA stops counting.

DANTE

Well . . . ?

VERONICA
(half-mumbled)
Something like thirty-six.

DANTE
WHAT? SOMETHING LIKE THIRTY-SIX?

VERONICA
Lower your voice!

DANTE
What the hell is that anyway, ''something like thirty-six''? Does that include me?

VERONICA
Um. Thirty-seven.

DANTE
I'M THIRTY-SEVEN?

VERONICA
(walking away)
I'm going to class.

DANTE
Thirty-seven?!
(to CUSTOMER)
My girlfriend sucked thirty-seven dicks!

CUSTOMER
In a row?

DANTE chases VERONICA down and grabs her by the door.

DANTE
Hey! Where are you going?!

VERONICA
Hey listen, jerk! Until today you never even knew how many guys I'd slept with, because you never even asked. And then you act all nonchalant about fucking twelve different girls. Well, I never had sex with twelve different guys!

DANTE
No, but you sucked enough dick!

VERONICA
Yeah, I went down on a few guys . . .

DANTE
A few?

VERONICA
. . . And one of those guys was you! The last one, I might add, which—if you're too stupid to comprehend—means that I've been faithful to you since we met! All the other guys I went with before I met you, so, if you want to have a complex about it, go ahead! But don't look at me like I'm the town whore, because you were plenty busy yourself, before you met me!

DANTE
(a bit more rational)
Well . . . why did you have to suck their dicks? Why didn't you just sleep with them, like any decent person?!

VERONICA
Because going down isn't a big deal! I used to like a guy, we'd make out, and sooner or later I'd go down on him. But I only had sex with the guys I loved.

DANTE
I feel sick.

VERONICA
(holds him)
I love you. Don't feel sick.

DANTE
Every time I kiss you now I'm going to taste thirty-six other guys.

VERONICA *violently lets go of him.*

VERONICA
I'm going to school. Maybe later you'll be a bit more rational.

DANTE
(pause)
Thirty-seven. I just can't . . .

VERONICA
Goodbye, Dante.

She exits in a huff. DANTE *stands there in silence for a moment. Then he swings the door open and yells out.*

DANTE
Try not to suck any more dicks on your way through the parking lot!

Two men who were walking in the opposite direction outside double back and head in the direction VERONICA *went.*

DANTE
HEY! HEY, YOU! GET BACK HERE!

Cut to:

INT: CONVENIENCE STORE. DAY

A videocassette encased in the customary black box flips repeatedly, held by an impatient grasp. The IMPATIENT CUSTOMER *glares at* DANTE. *Dante studies a copy of* Paradise Lost, *making a strong attempt at not noticing the glare.*

IMPATIENT CUSTOMER
(pissed off)
I thought that place was supposed to be opened at eleven o'clock? It's twenty after!

DANTE
I called his house twice already. He should be here soon.

IMPATIENT CUSTOMER
It's not like it's a demanding job. I'd like to get paid to sit on my ass and watch TV. The other day I walked in there and that sonofabitch was sleeping.

DANTE
I'm sure he wasn't sleeping.

IMPATIENT CUSTOMER

You calling me a liar?

DANTE

No; he was probably just resting his eyes.

IMPATIENT CUSTOMER

What the hell is that? Resting his eyes! It's not like he's some
goddamned air traffic controller!

DANTE

Actually, that's his night job.

IMPATIENT CUSTOMER

Such a wiseass. But go ahead. Crack wise. That's why you're
jockeying a register in some fucking local convenience store
instead of doing an honest day's work.
 (tosses tape on counter)
I got no more time to bullshit around waiting for that sonofabitch.
You make sure this gets back. The number's eight-
twelve—Wynarski. And I wanted to get a damn movie, too.

DANTE

If you'll just tell me the title of your rental choice, I'll have him
hold it for you.

IMPATIENT CUSTOMER
 (storming out)
Don't hurt yourself. I'm going to Big Choice Video
instead.

He storms out. Dante lifts a ring of keys from the counter.

DANTE
 (in a whisper)
You forgot your keys.

The half-filled trash can swallows the ring of keys. Cut to:

EXT: CONVENIENCE STORE. DAY

Another VIDEO-ANXIOUS CUSTOMER *leans against the video store
door. A hapless* RANDAL *drifts by and stops. He glances at the door,
peers inside, and gives the door a tug.*

                    V.A. CUSTOMER
The guy ain't here yet.

                    RANDAL
You're kidding. It's almost eleven-thirty!

                    V.A. CUSTOMER
I know. I've been here since eleven.

                    RANDAL
                 (kicks the door)
Man! I hate it when I can't rent videos!

                    V.A. CUSTOMER
I would've went to Big Choice, but the tape I want is right there
on the wall.

                    RANDAL
Which one?

                    V.A. CUSTOMER
Dental School.

                    RANDAL
You came for that too? That's the movie I came for.

                    V.A. CUSTOMER
I have first dibs.

                    RANDAL
Says who?

                    V.A. CUSTOMER
                 (suddenly snotty)
Says me. I've been here for half an hour. I'd call that first dibs.

                    RANDAL
Ain't gonna happen, my friend. I'm getting that tape.

                    V.A. CUSTOMER
Like hell you are!

                    RANDAL
I'll bet you twenty bucks you don't get to rent that tape.

Twenty bucks?

RANDAL

Twenty bucks.

V.A. CUSTOMER

All right, asshole, you're on.

RANDAL *walks away. The* VERY ANXIOUS CUSTOMER *stands like a sentry at post. The* IMPATIENT CUSTOMER *storms up.*

IMPATIENT CUSTOMER

You see a pair of keys lying around here somewhere?

Cut to:

INT: CONVENIENCE STORE. DAY

RANDAL *dances in, attempting a soft-shoe routine. He sees* DANTE *and stops dead, midshuffle.*

DANTE

You're late.

RANDAL

What the hell are you doing here? I thought you were playing hockey at one.

DANTE

The boss called. Arthur fell ill.

RANDAL

Why are the shutters closed?

DANTE

Someone jammed gum in the locks.

RANDAL

Bunch of savages in this town.

DANTE

That's what I said.

RANDAL

Shit, if I'd known you were working, I would've come even later.

A pile of videocassettes is plopped onto the counter, with a single key on top. RANDAL balances the pile of tapes on his head.

RANDAL

What time do you have to stay till?

DANTE

He assured me that he'd be here by twelve.

RANDAL

What smells like shoe polish?

DANTE

Go open the store.

Cut to:

EXT: CONVENIENCE STORE. DAY

The IMPATIENT CUSTOMER *stops* RANDAL.

IMPATIENT CUSTOMER

Hey—did you see a set of keys lying around here?

RANDAL

(as Short-round)

No time for love, Doctor Jones!

RANDAL *marches off. The* IMPATIENT CUSTOMER *stares after him.*

IMPATIENT CUSTOMER

Fucking kids.

The VERY ANXIOUS CUSTOMER *now sits on the ground, next to the video store door.* RANDAL *balances his burden and shoves the key into the lock. The* VERY ANXIOUS CUSTOMER *stares as* RANDAL *enters the store. The door closes behind him, only to be held ajar in a gentlemanly fashion a few moments later.* RANDAL *smiles. Cut to:*

INT: CONVENIENCE STORE. DAY

A coffee filter is shoved into the metal pan and someone heaps ground coffee on it. We've seen this same routine before. DANTE crosses back to his post, as RANDAL enters, tossing the key into the air happily and catching it. He picks the cat up.

> RANDAL
>
> Some guy just came in refusing to pay late fees. He said the store was closed for two hours yesterday. I tore up his membership.

> DANTE
>
> Shocking abuse of authority.

> RANDAL
>
> I'm a firm believer in the philosophy of a ruling class, especially since I rule.
> *(furtively)*
> Is the Pelican flying?

> DANTE
>
> Don't screw with it. It makes us look suspicious.

> RANDAL
>
> I can't stand a voyeur. I'll be back.

RANDAL heads toward the walk-in door. Cut to:

INT: BACK ROOM. DAY

POV: VCR

A far-away wall is the only thing we see, but mild gruntings give away an ascension of sorts. RANDAL'S head rises into view, as if he's climbing a ladder. He stops and looks into the lens.

POV: RANDAL
The PELICAN is a VCR that's hooked up to a surveillance camera. It records quickly. A hand reaches into the frame and shuts it off. Cut to:

INT: CONVENIENCE STORE. DAY

RANDAL pulls a soda from the cooler.

                              RANDAL
Want something to drink? I'm buying.

                           (OC) DANTE
No, thanks.

                              RANDAL
Who was on your phone this morning at about two-thirty? I was
trying to call for a half an hour.

                           (OC) DANTE
Why?

                              RANDAL
I wanted to use your car.

He walks by a row of snacks and grabs one without looking at it.

                              RANDAL
Snack cake?

*DANTE sits in his seat behind the register. RANDAL grabs a paper and
joins him behind the counter.*

                              DANTE
You don't want to know.

                              RANDAL
You called Caitlin again?!

                              DANTE
She called me.

                              RANDAL
Did you tell Veronica?

                              DANTE
One fight a day with Veronica is about all I can stomach, thanks.

                              RANDAL
What do you two fight about?

DANTE

I guess it's not really fighting. She just wants me to leave here, go
back to school, get some direction.

RANDAL
(opening paper)
I'll bet the most frequent topic of arguments is Caitlin Bree.

DANTE

You win.

RANDAL

I'm going to offer you some advice, my friend: let the past be the
past. Forget Caitlin Bree. You've been with Veronica for how long
now?

DANTE

Seven months.

RANDAL

Chick's nuts about you. How long did you date Caitlin?

DANTE

Five years.

RANDAL

Chick only made you nuts. She cheated on you how many times?

DANTE

Eight and a half.

RANDAL
(looks up from paper)
Eight and a half?

DANTE

Party at John K's—senior year. I get blitzed and pass out in his
bedroom. Caitlin comes in and dives all over me.

RANDAL

That's cheating?

DANTE

In the middle of it, she calls me Brad.

RANDAL

She called you Brad?

DANTE

She called me Brad.

RANDAL

That's not cheating. People say crazy shit during sex. One time, I called this girl ''Mom.''

DANTE

I hit the lights and she freaks. Turns out she thought I was Brad Michaelson.

RANDAL

What do you mean?

DANTE

She was supposed to meet Brad Michaelson in a bedroom. She picked the wrong one. She had no idea I was even at the party.

RANDAL

Oh, my God.

DANTE

Great story, isn't it?

RANDAL

That girl was vile to you.

DANTE

Interesting postscript to that story: Do you know who wound up going with Brad Michaelson in the other dark bedroom?

RANDAL

Your mother.

DANTE

Allan Harris.

RANDAL

Chess team Allan Harris?!

DANTE

The two moved to Idaho together after graduation. They raise sheep.

RANDAL

That's frightening.

DANTE

It takes different strokes to move the world.

RANDAL

In light of this lurid tale, I don't see how you could even romanticize your relationship with Caitlin—she broke your heart and inadvertently drove men to deviant lifestyles.

DANTE

Because there was a lot of good in our relationship.

RANDAL

Oh yeah.

DANTE

I'm serious. Aside from the cheating, we were a great couple. That's what high school's all about—algebra, bad lunch, and infidelity.

RANDAL

You think things would be any different now?

DANTE

They are. When she calls me now, she's a different person—she's frightened and vulnerable. She's about to finish college and enter the real world. That's got to be scary for anyone.

RANDAL
(suddenly recalling)
Oh shit, I've got to place an order.

DANTE

I'm talking to myself here.

RANDAL

No, no, I'm listening. She's leaving college, and . . . ?

DANTE

. . . and she's looking to me for support. And I think that this is leading our relationship to a new level.

RANDAL

What about Veronica?

DANTE

I think the arguments Veronica and I are having are some kind of manifestation of a subconscious desire to break away from her so that I can pursue the possibility of a more meaningful relationship with Caitlin.

RANDAL

Caitlin's on the same wave-length?

DANTE

I think it's safe to say yes.

RANDAL

Then I think all four of you had better sit down and talk it over.

DANTE

All four?

RANDAL

You, Veronica, Caitlin . . .
                (lays paper flat)
. . . and Caitlin's fiancé.

THE HEADLINE of the engagement announcement reads, BREE TO WED ASIAN DESIGN MAJOR.

Cut to:

INT: VIDEO STORE. DAY

RANDAL dials the phone. He holds a list in his hand.

RANDAL

Yes, I'd like to place an order, please . . . Thank you.

A MOTHER *and her* SMALL CHILD *approach the counter.*

MOTHER

Excuse me, but do you sell videotapes?

RANDAL

What were you looking for?

MOTHER

(smiling)

It's called *Happy Scrappy—The Hero Pup.*

SMALL CHILD

Happy Scrappy!

RANDAL

I'm on the phone with the distribution house now. Let me make
sure they have it. What's it called again?

MOTHER

Happy Scrappy—The Hero Pup.

SMALL CHILD

Happy Scrappy!

MOTHER

(more smiling)

She loves the tape.

RANDAL

Obviously.

(to phone)

Yes, hello; this is R.S.T. Video calling. Customer number four-
three-five-zero-two-nine. I'd like to place an order . . . Okay . . .

(reading from list)

I need one each of the following tapes: *Whisper in the Wind, To
Each His Own, Put it Where It Doesn't Belong, My Pipes Need
Cleaning, All Tit-Fucking, Volume Eight, I Need Your Cock, Ass-
Worshipping Rim-Jobbers, My Cunt and Eight Shafts, Cum Clean,
Cum-Gargling Naked Sluts, Cum Buns Three, Cumming in a
Sock, Cum on Eileen, Huge Black Cocks with Pearly White Cum,
Slam It Up My Too-Loose Ass, Ass Blasters in Outer Space,
Blowjobs by Betsy, Sucking Cock and Cunt, Finger My Ass, Play
with my Puss, Three on a Dildo, Girls Who Crave Cock, Girls*

Who Crave Cunt, Men Alone Two—The K.Y. Connection, Pink
Pussy Lips, and All Holes Filled with Hard Cock. Oh, and . . .
(to MOTHER)
What was the name of that movie?

MOTHER
(nearly dazed)
Happy Scrappy—The Hero Pup.

RANDAL
(to phone)
And a copy of *Happy Scrappy—The Hero Pup* . . . Okay, thanks.
(hangs up; to MOTHER)
Sixteen forty-nine. It'll be here Monday.

Silence. Then . . .

SMALL CHILD
Cunt!

Cut to:

INT: CONVENIENCE STORE. DAY

DANTE *carries a litter box to be dumped. He pauses midstride and lays
it on the ice cream chest.* DANTE *picks up the phone and looks at the
paper. He dials and waits.*

DANTE
Yes, I'd like to check on a misprint in today's edition . . . Today's
edition . . . It says "Bree to Wed Asian Design Major . . . No, no;
everything's spelled fine. I just wanted to know if the piece was a
misprint . . . I don't know, like a typographical error or
something . . .

A CUSTOMER *comes to the counter and waits. He looks at the litter box.
A black cat suddenly jumps into it and starts pawing around.*

(OC) DANTE
Maybe it's supposed to be Caitlin Bray, or Caitlin Bre, with one
e . . . I'm a curious party . . . A curious party . . .

DANTE *on the phone:*

DANTE

. . . I'm an ex-boyfriend . . . Well, it's just that we talk all the
time, and she never mentioned this engagement, which is why
I'm thinking maybe it's a misprint . . .

The CUSTOMER *watches as the cat takes a huge dump, leaning high on
its haunches to accommodate the stinky load.*

(OC) DANTE

. . . Are you sure? . . . Maybe there's like a vindictive printer
working for you . . .

DANTE *on the phone:*

DANTE

Meaning like someone who maybe—I don't know—asked her out
once and got shot down, and his revenge is throwing this bogus
article in when the paper went to press . . . Hello? . . . Hello?

DANTE *hangs up. He looks at the paper ruefully, shaking his head. He
then sniffs the air. Cut to:*

EXT: CONVENIENCE STORE. DAY

JAY, SILENT BOB *and* OLAF *lean against wall*

JAY

"Not in me." That's what she says. I gotta pull out and spank it
to get it on. So I blow a nut on her belly, and I get out of there,
just as my uncle walks in. It was such a close call. I tell you what,
though, I don't care if she is my cousin, I'm gonna knock those
boots again tonight.

TWO GIRLS *join them.*

JAY

Oh shit, look who it is. The human vacuum.

GIRL 1

Scumbag. What are you doing?

JAY

Nothing. Just hanging out, talking with Silent Bob and his cousin.

                    GIRL 1
                (to SILENT BOB)
He's your cousin?

                     JAY
Check this out, he's from Russia.

                    GIRL 1
No way.

                     JAY
I swear to God. Silent Bob, am I lying?

SILENT BOB *shakes his head:*

                     JAY
See? And Silent Bob never told a lie in his life.

                    GIRL 2
What part of Russia?

                     JAY
I don't fucking know. What am I, his biographer?
                (to OLAF)
Olaf, what part of Russia are you from?

OLAF *looks quizzically at* SILENT BOB.

                 SILENT BOB
                (in Russian)
Home.

                    OLAF
                (comprehending)
Moscow.

                    GIRL 1
He only speaks Russian?

                     JAY
He knows some English, but he can't not speak it good like we do.

                    GIRL 2
Is he staying here?

                              JAY

He's moving to the big city next week. He wants to be a metal
singer.

                            GIRL 1

No way!

                              JAY

Swear.
                          (to OLAF)

Olaf, metal!

OLAF *makes a metal face.*

                              JAY

That's his fucking metal face.
                          (to OLAF)

Olaf, girls nice?

OLAF *looks the girls up and down.*

                             OLAF

Skrelnick.

                              JAY
                           (laughs)

That's fucked up.

                            GIRL 1

What did he say?

                              JAY

I don't know, man. He's a fucking character.

                            GIRL 2

He really wants to play metal?

                              JAY

He's got his own band in Moscow. It's called ''Fuck Your Yankee
Blue Jeans'' or something like that.

                            GIRL 1

That doesn't sound metal.

                    JAY
You gotta hear him sing.
                    (to OLAF*)*
Olaf, ''Berserker''!

OLAF *laughs and shakes his head.*

                    JAY
Come on, man, ''Berserker''!

                    GIRL 2
Does he sing in English or Russian?

                    JAY
English.
                    (to OLAF*)*
Come on, ''Berserker''! Girls think sexy.

                    OLAF
                    (relents)
Da. Da.

                    JAY
He's gonna sing it. This is too funny.

                    OLAF
                    (in broken English)
MY LOVE FOR YOU IS LIKE A TRUCK BERSERKER!
WOULD YOU LIKE SOME MAKING FUCK?
BERSERKER!

                    JAY
                    (laughing)
That's fucking funny, man!

                    GIRL 1
Did he say ''making fuck''?

                    JAY
Wait, there's more.
                    (to OLAF*)*
Olaf: sing . . .
                    (makes pot-smoking face)

OLAF
(nods in understanding)
MY LOVE FOR YOU IS LIKE A ROCK
BERSERKER!
WOULD YOU LIKE TO SMOKE SOME POT?
BERSERKER!

OLAF *busts a crimson metal sneer and cackles deeply. Cut to:*

INT: VIDEO STORE. DAY

RANDAL *leans back in his chair, staring up at the TV. The theme to* Star Wars *plays. He stands, points the remote, clicks the TV off, and ponders. Cut to:*

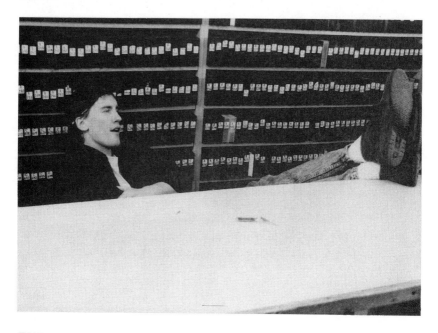

EXT: VIDEO STORE. DAY

RANDAL *locks the door and walks away, while* OLAF *sings for the small crowd.*

OLAF
MY LOVE FOR YOU IS TICKING CLOCK
BERSERKER!
WOULD YOU LIKE TO SUCK MY COCK?
BERSERKER!

Cut to:

INT: CONVENIENCE STORE. DAY

DANTE *is tugging at a can of Pringles potato chips. The can is stuck on a* MAN'S *hand.*

DANTE

You hold the counter and I'll pull.

MAN

Usually I just turn the can upside down.

DANTE
(pulling)

Maybe we should soap up your hand or something.

MAN
(straining)

They oughta put some kind of warning on these cans, like they do with cigarettes.

DANTE

I think it's coming now . . .

The can pops off and DANTE *staggers back a few steps. The man rubs his hand.*

MAN

Thanks. I thought I was gonna have to go to the hospital.

DANTE

I'll throw this out. Precautionary measure.

MAN

It stings a little.

DANTE

A word of advice: Sometimes it's best to let those hard to reach chips go.

DANTE *steps behind the counter.*

MAN

Thanks.

The MAN *exits as* RANDAL *enters.* DANTE *throws the canister away.*

DANTE

Do you know that article is accurate? Caitlin's really getting
married!

RANDAL

You know what I just watched?

DANTE

Me pulling a can off some moron's fist.

RANDAL

Return of the Jedi.

DANTE

Didn't you hear me? Caitlin really is getting married.

RANDAL

Which did you like better: *Jedi* or *The Empire Strikes Back?*

DANTE
(exasperated)

Empire.

RANDAL

Blasphemy.

DANTE

Empire had the better ending: Luke gets his hand cut off, and
finds out Vader's his father; Han gets frozen and taken away by
Boba Fett. It ends on such a down note. And that's life—a series
of down endings. All *Jedi* had was a bunch of Muppets.

RANDAL

There was something else going on in *Jedi.* I never noticed it until
today.

RANDAL *follows* DANTE *as he cleans up around the store.*

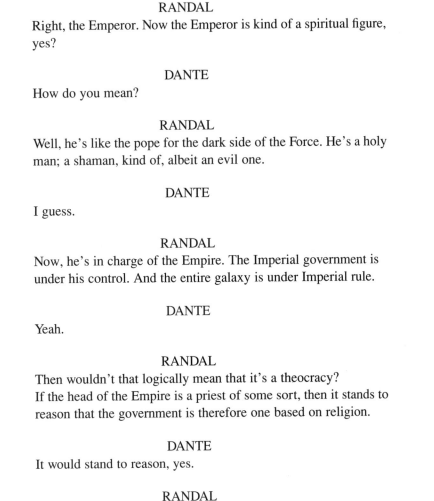

DANTE

What's that?

RANDAL

All right, Vader's boss . . .

DANTE

The Emperor.

RANDAL

Right, the Emperor. Now the Emperor is kind of a spiritual figure, yes?

DANTE

How do you mean?

RANDAL

Well, he's like the pope for the dark side of the Force. He's a holy man; a shaman, kind of, albeit an evil one.

DANTE

I guess.

RANDAL

Now, he's in charge of the Empire. The Imperial government is under his control. And the entire galaxy is under Imperial rule.

DANTE

Yeah.

RANDAL

Then wouldn't that logically mean that it's a theocracy?
If the head of the Empire is a priest of some sort, then it stands to reason that the government is therefore one based on religion.

DANTE

It would stand to reason, yes.

RANDAL

Hence, the Empire was a fascist theocracy, and the rebel forces were therefore battling religious persecution.

DANTE

More or less.

RANDAL

The only problem is that at no point in the series did I ever hear
Leia or any of the rebels declare a particular religious belief.

DANTE

I think they were Catholics.

A BLUE-COLLAR MAN half enters the door.

BLUE-COLLAR MAN

Are you open?

DANTE

Yeah. Come in.

He goes to the coffee machine and makes a cup of joe.

RANDAL

You know what else I noticed in *Jedi*?

DANTE

There's more?

RANDAL

So they build another Death Star, right?

DANTE

Yeah.

RANDAL

Now the first one they built was completed and fully operational
before the Rebels destroyed it.

DANTE

Luke blew it up. Give credit where it's due.

RANDAL

And the second one was still being built when they blew it up.

DANTE

Compliments of Lando Calrissian.

RANDAL

Something just never sat right with me the second time they destroyed it. I could never put my finger on it—something just wasn't right.

DANTE

And you figured it out?

RANDAL

Well, the thing is, the first Death Star was manned by the Imperial army—storm troopers, dignitaries—the only people onboard were Imperials.

DANTE

Basically.

RANDAL

So when they blew it up, no prob. Evil is punished.

DANTE

And the second time around . . . ?

RANDAL

The second time around, it wasn't even finished yet. They were still under construction.

DANTE

So?

RANDAL

A construction job of that magnitude would require a helluva lot more manpower than the Imperial army had to offer. I'll bet there were independent contractors working on that thing: plumbers, aluminum siders, roofers.

DANTE

Not just Imperials, is what you're getting at.

RANDAL

Exactly. In order to get it built quickly and quietly they'd hire anybody who could do the job. Do you think the average storm trooper knows how to install a toilet main? All they know is killing and white uniforms.

DANTE

All right, so even if independent contractors are working on the Death Star, why are you uneasy with its destruction?

RANDAL

All those innocent contractors hired to do a job were killed—casualties of a war they had nothing to do with.
(notices Dante's *confusion)*
All right, look—you're a roofer, and some juicy government contract comes your way; you got the wife and kids and the two-story in suburbia—this is a government contract, which means all sorts of benefits. All of a sudden these left-wing militants blast you with lasers and wipe out everyone within a three-mile radius. You didn't ask for that. You have no personal politics. You're just trying to scrape out a living.

The BLUE-COLLAR MAN *joins them.*

BLUE-COLLAR MAN

Excuse me. I don't mean to interrupt, but what were you talking about?

RANDAL

The ending of *Return of the Jedi.*

DANTE

My friend is trying to convince me that any contractors working on the uncompleted Death Star were innocent victims when the space station was destroyed by the rebels.

BLUE-COLLAR MAN

Well, I'm a contractor myself. I'm a roofer . . .
(digs into pocket and produces business card)
Dunn and Reddy Home Improvements. And speaking as a roofer, I can say that a roofer's personal politics come heavily into play when choosing jobs.

RANDAL

Like when?

BLUE-COLLAR MAN

Three months ago I was offered a job up in the hills. A beautiful house with tons of property. It was a simple reshingling job, but

I was told that if it was finished within a day, my price would be doubled. Then I realized whose house it was.

DANTE

Whose house was it?

BLUE-COLLAR MAN

Dominick Bambino's.

RANDAL

"Babyface" Bambino? The gangster?

BLUE-COLLAR MAN

The same. The money was right, but the risk was too big. I knew who he was, and based on that, I passed the job on to a friend of mine.

DANTE

Based on personal politics.

BLUE-COLLAR MAN

Right. And that week, the Foresci family put a hit on Babyface's house. My friend was shot and killed. He wasn't even finished shingling.

RANDAL

No way!

BLUE-COLLAR MAN
(paying for coffee)
I'm alive because I knew there were risks involved taking on that particular client. My friend wasn't so lucky.
(pauses to reflect)
You know, any contracter willing to work on that Death Star knew the risks. If they were killed, it was their own fault. A roofer listens to this . . .
(taps his heart)
not his wallet.

The BLUE-COLLAR MAN *exits.* DANTE *and* RANDAL *remain respectfully quiet for a moment. An angry* WOMAN *opens the door and pokes her head in.*

Is that video store open or not?

Cut to:

INT: VIDEO STORE. DAY

RANDAL *reads a newspaper. An* INDECISIVE CUSTOMER *studies the two rental choices she holds. She looks from one movie to the other, repeatedly.*

INDECISIVE CUSTOMER
(attempting to solicit help)
They say so much, but they never tell you if it's any good.

RANDAL *hardly stirs and continues to read his paper. The* INDECISIVE CUSTOMER *half turns to see if her comment was even heard. She tries again, but this time with a different approach.*

INDECISIVE CUSTOMER
Are either of these any good?

RANDAL *continues to read. The* INDECISIVE CUSTOMER *tries harder, then louder and more direct:*

Sir!

RANDAL *continues to read.*

RANDAL
(flatly)
What.

The INDECISIVE CUSTOMER *holds up her rental choices.*

INDECISIVE CUSTOMER
(politely)
Are either of these any good?

RANDAL, *as always, reads on.*

RANDAL
(again, flatly)
I don't watch movies.

The INDECISIVE CUSTOMER *is a tad flabbergasted, but not put off.*

INDECISIVE CUSTOMER
Well, have you heard anything about either of them?

RANDAL *does his level best to not get involved.*

RANDAL
(reading)
No.

The INDECISIVE CUSTOMER *challenges him.*

INDECISIVE CUSTOMER
(in disbelief)
You've never heard anybody say anything about either movie?

(OC) RANDAL
I find it's best to stay out of other people's affairs.

INDECISIVE CUSTOMER
(with a new determination)
Well, how about these two movies?
(holds up the same two)

RANDAL *continues to read his paper, not looking up.*

RANDAL
They suck.

The INDECISIVE CUSTOMER *smirks smugly at* RANDAL *and his paper. She has caught him.*

INDECISIVE CUSTOMER
I just held up the same two movies. You're not even paying attention.

RANDAL
No, I wasn't.

INDECISIVE CUSTOMER

I don't think your manager would appreciate . . .

RANDAL

(turning the page)

I don't appreciate your ruse, ma'am.

INDECISIVE CUSTOMER

I beg your pardon!

RANDAL

(reading on)

Your ruse. Your cunning attempt to trick me.

INDECISIVE CUSTOMER

(defending herself)

I only pointed out that you weren't paying any attention to what I was saying.

RANDAL

(turning page and reading)

I hope it feels good.

INDECISIVE CUSTOMER

You hope what feels good?

RANDAL

I hope it feels so good to be right. There is nothing more exhilarating than pointing out the shortcomings of others, is there?

The INDECISIVE CUSTOMER *wears a face that belies utter disbelief in the audacity of this most lackadaisical video clerk. The unmoving newspaper illustrates the total disinterest of the news-hungry* RANDAL. *The* INDECISIVE CUSTOMER *shakes her head in digust and throws the movies back onto the wall.*

INDECISIVE CUSTOMER

(in a huff)

Well this is the last time I ever rent here . . .

RANDAL

You'll be missed.

INDECISIVE CUSTOMER
(losing it altogether)
Screw you!

She storms out. RANDAL is offended. He hops over the counter and whips the door open.

RANDAL
(calling after her)
You're not allowed to rent here anymore!

RANDAL closes the door and stands there, momentarily, totally appalled by her exiting remark, then shakes his head.

Screw me!

He reaches behind the counter and grabs a ring of keys. Exiting, he locks the door behind him from outside, gives it a tug to ensure its security, and storms off in the opposite direction from the woman. Cut to:

INT: CONVENIENCE STORE. DAY

DANTE is staring, open-mouthed, at something OC. RANDAL hurls the door open and immediately launches into his tirade.

RANDAL
You'll never believe what this unruly customer just said . . .

DANTE
(a hand up to urge him to hush)
Wait.

RANDAL
(looking around)
She's in here?

DANTE
This guy is going through all of the eggs. Look.

An ODD MAN sits on the floor, surrounded by cartons of eggs, all opened. He grabs a carton from the cooler case, pops it open, and examines each egg carefully.

                        (OC) DANTE
        This has been going on for twenty minutes.

RANDAL *and* DANTE *study the* OC *oddity.*

                         RANDAL
        What's he looking for?

                          DANTE
        He said he has to find a perfect dozen.

                         RANDAL
        Perfect dozen.

                          DANTE
        Each egg has to be perfect.

                         RANDAL
        The quest isn't going well?

                          DANTE
        Obviously not. Look at all the cartons that didn't make the grade.

The ODD MAN *holds an egg up to the light and studies it from several
different angles.*

                       (OC) RANDAL
        Why doesn't he just mix and match?

                       (OC) DANTE
        I told him that and he yelled at me.

RANDAL *snickers at his friend.*

                         RANDAL
        What did he say?

                          DANTE
        He said it was important to have standards. He said nobody has
        pride anymore.

                         RANDAL
        It's not like you laid the eggs yourself.

DANTE

I'll give him five more minutes and then I'm calling the cops. I don't need this, man. I'm not even supposed to be here today.

A SMOKER *steps in.*

SMOKER

Two packs of cigarettes.

Dante manages to break his study of the OC *oddity and searches for the smokes. The smoker glances at* RANDAL *and then at the* OC *oddity.*

The ODD MAN *is spinning an egg on the floor. The* SMOKER *looks at* RANDAL.

RANDAL
(still staring at the ODD MAN)
I'm as puzzled as you.

SMOKER
(paying DANTE)
I've actually seen it before.

DANTE

You know him?

SMOKER

No, I've seen that behavior before. Looking for the perfect carton of eggs, right?

RANDAL
(a bit astonished)
Yeah. How'd you know?

SMOKER

I'll bet you a million bucks that the guy's a guidance counselor.

DANTE

Why do you say that?

SMOKER

I was in Food City last year when the same thing happened, different guy though. Stock boy told me that the guy had been looking through the eggs for like half an hour, doing all sorts of endurance tests and shit. I ask the kid how come nobody called the manager, and he says it happens twice a week, sometimes more.

RANDAL

Get out of here.

SMOKER

I kid you not. They call it Shell Shock. Only happens with guidance counselors for some reason. The kid said they used to make a big deal about it, but there's no point.

The ODD MAN *places a handkerchief over an egg on the floor. He quickly whisks the handkerchief away to reveal the egg still sitting on the floor.*

(OC) SMOKER

He said they always pay for whatever they break and they never bother anybody.

DANTE, RANDAL *and the* SMOKER *stare at the* OC *man.*

DANTE

Why guidance counselors?

SMOKER

If your job served as little purpose as theirs, wouldn't you lose it, too?

RANDAL

Come to think of it, my guidance counselor was kind of worthless.

SMOKER
(grabbing matches)
See? It's important to have a job that makes a difference, boys. That's why I kill Chinamen for the railroad.

Cut to:

INT: CONVENIENCE STORE. DAY

POV RANDAL: THE EMPTY COUNTER

And then a LITTLE GIRL *comes into view, smiling and holding money. She can't be any more than five.*

LITTLE GIRL
(innocently)
Can I have a pack of cigarettes?

RANDAL, *without looking up from his magazine, completes the transaction.* THE LITTLE GIRL *puts a cigarette in her mouth.* RANDAL *hands her matches.* DANTE *returns to the counter as the girl skips away. Dante holds a price gun.*

DANTE
Did you ever notice all the prices end in nine? Damn, that's eerie.

RANDAL
You know how much money the average jizz-mopper makes per hour?

DANTE
What's a jizz-mopper?

RANDAL
He's the guy in those nudie-booth joints who cleans up after each guy that jerks off.

DANTE
Nudie booth?

RANDAL
Nudie booth. You've never been in a nudie booth?

DANTE
I guess not.

A female CUSTOMER *pops items onto the counter.* DANTE *rings her up.*

RANDAL
Oh, it's great. You step into this little booth and there's this window between you and this naked woman, and she puts on this little show for like ten bucks.

DANTE
What kind of show?

RANDAL

Think of the weirdest, craziest shit you'd like to see chicks do.
These chicks do it all. They insert things into any opening in their
body . . . *any* opening.

(to customer)

He's led a very sheltered life.

DANTE

(indicating CUSTOMER)

Can we talk about this later?

RANDAL

The jizz-mopper's job is to clean up the booths afterward, because
practically everybody shoots a load against the window, and I
don't know if you know this or not, but cum leaves streaks if you
don't clean it right away.

CUSTOMER

(grabbing her bag, disgusted)

This is the last time I come to this place.

DANTE

Excuse me?

CUSTOMER

Using filthy language in front of the customers . . . you should
both get fired.

DANTE

We're sorry, ma'am. We got a little carried away.

CUSTOMER

Well, I don't know if sorry can make up for it. I found your
remarks highly offensive.

The CUSTOMER *stands silently, awaiting something.*

RANDAL

Well, if you think that's offensive . . .

RANDAL *flips open the magazine's centerfold—a graphic picture of a
woman with her vaginal lips and anus spread wide open.*

RANDAL

. . . then check this out. I think you can see her kidneys.

RANDAL *checks out the centerfold wistfully.* DANTE *frantically apologizes to the rapidly exiting* CUSTOMER.

DANTE

Ma'am, ma'am, I'm sorry! Please, wait a second, ma'am . . .

The CUSTOMER *is gone.* DANTE'S *pursuit stops at the counter.* DANTE *turns on* RANDAL.

DANTE

Why do you do things like that? You know she's going to come back and tell the boss.

RANDAL

Who cares? That lady's an asshole. Everybody that comes in here is way too uptight. This job would be great if it wasn't for the fucking customers.

DANTE

I'm gonna hear it tomorrow.

RANDAL

You gotta loosen up, my friend. You'd feel a hell of a lot better if you'd rip into the occasional customer.

DANTE

What for? They don't bother me if I don't bother them.

RANDAL

Liar! Tell me there aren't customers that annoy the piss out of you on a daily basis.

DANTE

There aren't.

RANDAL

How can you lie like that? Why don't you vent? Vent your frustration. Come on, who pisses you off?

                    DANTE
                  (reluctantly)
It's not really anyone per se, it's more of separate groupings.

                    RANDAL
Let's hear it.

                    DANTE
                    (pause)
The milkmaids.

                    RANDAL
The milkmaids?

INSERT: MILK HANDLER

A WOMAN pulls out gallon after gallon, looking deep into the cooler for that perfect container of milk.

                  (OC) DANTE
The women that go through every gallon of milk looking for a later date. As if somewhere—beyond all the other gallons—is a container of milk that won't go bad for like a decade.

END INSERT

                    RANDAL
You know who I can do without? I could do without the people in the video store.

                    DANTE
Which ones?

                    RANDAL
All of them.

MONTAGE INSERT #1/VIDEO JERKS

A series of people addressing the camera, asking the dumb questions.

                    FIRST
What would you get for a six-year-old boy who chronically wets his bed?

SECOND
(in front of stocked new release shelf)
Do you have any new movies in?

THIRD
Do you have that one with the guy who was in that movie that was out last year?

END INSERT

RANDAL
And they never rent quality flicks; they always pick the most intellectually devoid movie on the rack.

MONTAGE INSERT #2/"Ooooh! . . ."

An identical series of customers finding their ideal choices.

FIRST
Ooooh! *Home Alone*!

SECOND
Ooooh! *Hook*!

THIRD
Ooooh! *Navy Seals*!

END INSERT

RANDAL
It's like in order to join, they have to have an IQ less than their shoe size.

DANTE
You think you get stupid questions? You should hear the barrage of stupid questions I get.

MONTAGE INSERT #3/DUMB QUESTIONS

A series of people standing in various locations throughout the convenience store, asking truly dumb questions.

FIRST
(holding coffee)
What do you mean there's no ice? You mean I've gotta drink this
coffee hot?!

SECOND
(holding up item from clearly marked $.99 display)
How much?

THIRD
(peeking in door)
Do you sell hubcaps?

END INSERT

RANDAL
See? You vented. Don't you feel better now?

DANTE
No.

RANDAL
Why not?

DANTE
Because my ex-girlfriend is getting married.

RANDAL
Jesus, you got a one-track mind. It's always
Caitlin, Caitlin, Caitlin . . .

DANTE
(jerking head toward door)
Veronica!

DANTE *gives* RANDAL *a shove to shut him up.* VERONICA *enters the
store, carrying books and something covered with aluminum foil.*

VERONICA
What happened to home by twelve?

DANTE *is suddenly by her side, taking the books from under her arm.*

DANTE

He still hasn't shown up. Why aren't you in class?

VERONICA

Lit 101 got canceled, so I stopped home and brought you some
lunch.

DANTE

What is it?

VERONICA

Peanut butter and jelly with the crusts cut off. What do you think
it is? It's lasagne.

DANTE

Really?
                    (kisses her forehead)
You're the best.

VERONICA

I'm glad you've calmed down a bit.
                    (to RANDAL)
Hi, Randal.

(OC) RANDAL
(exaggeratively impressed)

Thirty-seven!

DANTE
(to OC)

Shut up!
                    (to VERONICA)
Yes, I've calmed down. I'm still not happy about it, but I've been
able to deal.

RANDAL *makes loud slurping noises from OC.*

DANTE
(to OC)
Why don't you go back to the video store?

RANDAL *walks past the two, and pats VERONICA on the head. He exits.*

VERONICA

You had to tell him.

DANTE

I had to tell someone. He put it into perspective.

VERONICA

What did he say?

DANTE

At least he wasn't thirty-six.

VERONICA

And that made you feel better?

DANTE

And he said most of them are college guys I've never met or seen.

VERONICA

The ostrich syndrome: if you don't see it . . .

DANTE

it isn't there. Yes.

VERONICA

Thank you for being rational.

DANTE

Thank you for the lasagne.

VERONICA

You couldn't get these shutters open?

DANTE

I called a locksmith and he said the earliest he could get here is tomorrow.

VERONICA

Bummer. Well, I've gotta head back for the one-thirty class.

DANTE

What time do you get finished?

VERONICA

Eight. But I have a sorority meeting till nine, so I'll be back before you close. Can we go out and get some coffee?

DANTE

Sure.

VERONICA

Good.
(kisses him)
I'll see you when you close, then. Enjoy the lasagne.

She exits. DANTE leans against the magazine rack with his lasagne, contemplative. RANDAL pops his head in and makes the loud slurping noise again. Cut to:

INT: VIDEO STORE. DAY

RANDAL is recommending titles to potential customers.

RANDAL

All right, now if you're really feeling dangerous tonight, then *Smokey and the Bandit Three* is the movie you must rent.

CUSTOMER
(studying box)
This doesn't even have Burt Reynolds in it.

RANDAL

Hey, neither did *ET*; but that was a great movie, right?

DANTE opens the door and leans in.

DANTE

Can you come next door? I gotta make a phone call.

RANDAL
(to DANTE)
Smokey Three: thumbs up, am I right?

DANTE

The best Burtless movie ever made.

DANTE exits. RANDAL gives his customers the what-did-I-tell-you look. Cut to:

INT: CONVENIENCE STORE. DAY

THE CAT *lies on the counter. Pull back to reveal* RANDAL *as he rings up an order. The* CUSTOMER *pets the cat, smiling.*

> CUSTOMER
> Awww, he's so cute. What's his name?

> RANDAL
> Lenin's Tomb.

Dolly over to DANTE, *on the phone.*

> DANTE
> Hello, is Mr. Snyder there? This is Dante . . . Did he say if he was on his way here? . . . Here . . . The convenience store . . . I know, but the other guy called out this morning and Mr. Snyder asked me to cover until he got here. He said he'd be here by noon, but it's one-thirty now, so I . . . Excuse me . . . Vermont!? . . . No, that can't be; I talked to him this morning . . . He left at what time? . . . He really went to Vermont? . . . When the hell was someone going to tell me? . . . He promised he was coming by noon! . . . Jesus . . . When does he get back?! . . . TUESDAY! . . . You've gotta be fucking kidding me! . . . I've got a hockey game at two, and the fucking shutters are jammed closed, and he's in Vermont? . . . I'm not even supposed to be here today!!
> *(deep sigh)*
> So I'm stuck here till closing? . . . This is just great . . . I just can't believe . . . I'm sorry, I didn't mean to yell at you . . . No . . . No, I'll be all right . . . Well, that's all I can do, right? . . . Thanks.

He hangs up. RANDAL *joins him.*

> RANDAL
> Vermont?

> DANTE
> Can you believe this?!

> RANDAL
> He didn't mention it when he called you this morning?

DANTE

Not a fucking word! Slippery shit!

RANDAL

So, what—you're stuck here all day?

DANTE

FUCK!

RANDAL

Why'd you apologize?

DANTE

What?

RANDAL

I heard you apologize. Why? You have every right in the world to be mad.

DANTE

I know.

RANDAL

That seems to be the leitmotif in your life; ever backing down.

DANTE

I don't back down.

RANDAL

Yes, you do. You always back down. You assume blame that isn't yours, you come in when called as opposed to enjoying your day off, you buckle like a belt.

DANTE

You know what pisses me off the most?

RANDAL

The fact that I'm right about your buckling?

DANTE

I'm going to miss the game.

RANDAL

Because you buckled.

DANTE

Would you shut the hell up with that shit? It's not helping.

RANDAL

Don't yell at me, pal.

DANTE

Sorry.

RANDAL

See? There you go again.

DANTE

I can't believe I'm going to miss the game!

RANDAL

At least we're stuck here together.

DANTE

You've got a customer.

RANDAL *walks away.*

(OC) RANDAL

What? What do you want?!

DANTE *shakes his head in frustration and picks up the phone again.*

DANTE

Sanford? Dante . . . I can't play today . . . I'm stuck at work . . . I
know I'm not scheduled, but—just forget it. I can't play . . .
Neither can Randal. . . . He's working too. . . .

RANDAL *comes back.* DANTE *rolls his eyes to the ceiling.*

DANTE
(getting an idea)
Wait a second. Do we have to play at the park? . . . Hold on . . .
(to RANDAL)
Do you feel limber?

Cut to:

INT: CONVENIENCE STORE. DAY

TAPE is rolled around the top of a stick. Laces are pulled tightly. An orange ball is slapped back and forth by a blade. The HOCKEY PLAYERS fill the convenience store. Some sit on the floor or lean against the coolers, but all are either preparing or practicing. RANDAL enters, wearing his equipment. DANTE skates to his side.

> DANTE
> *(lifting his foot)*
Pull my laces tighter.

> RANDAL
> *(drops mitt and pulls laces)*
I've gotta tell you, my friend: this is one of the ballsiest moves I've ever been privy to. I never would have thought you capable of such blatant disregard of store policy.

> DANTE
I told him I had a game today. It's his own fault.

> RANDAL
No argument here. Insubordination rules.

> DANTE
I just want to play hockey like I was scheduled to.

SANFORD skates up and skids to a halt.

> SANFORD
Dante, let me grab a Gatorade.

> DANTE
If you grab a Gatorade, then everyone's going to grab one.

> SANFORD
So?

> DANTE
So? So nobody's going to want to pay for these Gatorades.

SANFORD

What do you care? Hey, what smells like shoe polish?

DANTE

I've got a responsibility here. I can't let everybody grab free drinks.

SANFORD

What responsibility? You're closing the fucking store to play hockey.

RANDAL

He's blunt, but he's got a point.

DANTE

At least let me maintain some semblance of managerial control here.

SANFORD

All I'm saying is if you're going to be insubordinate, you should go the full nine and not pussy out when it comes to free refreshments.

RANDAL

He's right. As if we're suddenly gonna have a run on Gatorade.

SANFORD

Fuckin-A.

DANTE

All right. Jesus, you fuckers are pushy.

SANFORD

Hey man, I hear Caitlin's marrying an Asian drum major.

RANDAL

Design major.

DANTE

Can we not talk about this?

SANFORD

Fine by me. But you're living in denial and suppressing rage.
(*skating away; to all*)
Dante said we can all drink free Gatorade.

A laid-back hurrah is heard.

RANDAL

Are you gonna lock the store?

DANTE

I don't know. You going to lock the video store?

RANDAL

Look who you're asking here. How're we gonna block off the street?

DANTE

We're not playing in the street.

RANDAL

Then where're we gonna play?

Cut to:

EXT: CONVENIENCE STORE. DAY

The sign on the door reads:

TEMPORARILY CLOSED. BE OPENED AFTER FIRST PERIOD.

The PLAYERS *ascend a ladder adjacent to the door, one by one.* ON THE ROOF *they jump off the ladder and skate around. More players join them. From across the street we get the full, odd perspective: a store with many men gliding around on the roof.*

On the roof DANTE *skates and passes with another player.* REDDING *stretches, leaning against the sign.* RANDAL *pulls his mask on and slaps his glove, urging a shot.* SANFORD *skates in and takes a shot, which* RANDAL *blocks.* JAY *and* SILENT BOB *deal to a player: he drops money over the ledge and* JAY *throws up a dime bag.* DANTE *holds a ball in the center of the court.*

DANTE

Ready?

PLAYERS *take positions.* SANFORD *comes to the center and holds the ball in drop position.* DANTE *and* REDDING *face off, and the ball is in play.*

The game begins as the players engage in a savage ballet. Faces are smashed with sticks, slide tackles are made, shots are taken, CU's of various players included.

INACTIVE PLAYERS *call out encouragement and slander from the sidelines. More game playing including both goalies getting scored on and more face-offs.*

Below, a CUSTOMER *tugs on the convenience store door. He reads the sign and then backs up into the street, attempting to peer over the ledge. Above, the game continues.*

Below, the CUSTOMER *shifts from one foot to the other impatiently. He grabs the ladder and quickly ascends.*

Above, from over the ledge of the roof, we see the head of the customer peek. Skating feet pass rapidly before him, and he watches for a moment before calling out.

CUSTOMER

When's this period over?

SOMEONE O.C.

Eight more minutes!

CUSTOMER

Are you shitting me? I want to get cigarettes!

DANTE *skids to the sidelines.*

DANTE
(out of breath)

If you can just wait a few more minutes.

CUSTOMER

Fuck that! I'm gonna break my crazy neck on this ladder!

(OC) SOMEONE
Dante! Where are you?!

CUSTOMER
He's busy!

DANTE *starts to skate away.*

DANTE
I'll be right back. It's almost over.

He jumps back into the game.

CUSTOMER
What the fuck is this?! I want some service!

(OC) DANTE
In a second!

CUSTOMER
Fuck in a second! This is . . . Look at you! You can't even pass!

(OC) DANTE
I can pass!

CUSTOMER
How 'bout covering point!? You suck!

DANTE *skids back to the sidelines to address the* CUSTOMER.

DANTE
Who are you to make assessments?

CUSTOMER
I'll assess all I want!

(OC) SOMEONE
DANTE! ARE YOU IN OR OUT!

CUSTOMER
(to O.C. SOMEONE)
Don't pass to this guy! He sucks!
(to DANTE)
You suck!

DANTE

Like you're better!

CUSTOMER

I can whip your ass.

Below, a WOMAN pulls at the door. She peers into the store, face against the glass.

(OC) DANTE

That's easy to say from over here.

(OC) CUSTOMER

Give me a stick, pretty boy! I'll knock your fucking teeth out and pass all over your ass.

The WOMAN backs up and, shielding her eyes, looks toward the roof.

WOMAN

Is the convenience store open?

Above, DANTE and the CUSTOMER shout down at the OC WOMAN.

DANTE AND CUSTOMER
(simultaneously)

NO!

DANTE
(to CUSTOMER)
There's a stick over there. You're shooting against the goal.
(to the court)
REDDING! COME OFF AND LET THIS FUCK ON!

A new face-off pits DANTE against the CUSTOMER. The ball drops between the two and DANTE gets flattened. The CUSTOMER winds up and takes a hard shot. The ball sails off the court, through the air, and into a faraway yard. DANTE calls to the sidelines.

DANTE

Give me another ball.

(OC) SOMEONE

There are no more.

DANTE

What the fuck are you talking about? How many balls did you
bring?

SANFORD *skates up to him.*

SANFORD
(counting)
There was the orange ball . . . and the orange ball.

DANTE *scrambles to the ledge and calls over.*

DANTE
Are there any balls down there?!

(OC) JAY
'Bout the biggest pair you ever seen! NYNNE!!

DANTE *looks around, hyperventilating.*

DANTE
You only brought one ball?!

SANFORD
I thought Redding had like three balls!

(OC) REDDING
I thought Dante had the balls.

DANTE
Nobody has another ball?

SANFORD

Shit!

DANTE
We get . . . what . . . twelve minutes of game, and it's over? Fuck!
Fuck! Fuck! Fuck!!
(pause; rubs head)
I'm not even supposed to be here today!

DANTE *skates off.*

SANFORD
We still get free Gatorade, right?

CUT TO:

INT: CONVENIENCE STORE. DAY

DANTE *standing on a ladder, replaces a fluorescent light. An* OLD MAN *joins him at the foot of the ladder.*

OLD MAN
Be careful.

DANTE
I'm trying.

OLD MAN
You know the insides of those are filled with stuff that gives you cancer.

DANTE
So I'm told.

OLD MAN
I had a friend that used to chew glass for a living. In the circus.

The light in place, DANTE *descends the ladder and closes it.*

DANTE
And he got cancer by chewing fluorescent bulb glass . . . ?

OLD MAN
No, he got hit by a bus.

DANTE
(confused)
Oh . . . Can I help you?

OLD MAN
Well, that depends. Do you have a bathroom?

DANTE
Um . . . yeah, but it's for employees only.

OLD MAN

I understand, but can I use it. I'm not that young anymore, so I'm kind of . . . you know . . . incontinent.

DANTE

Uh . . . sure. Go ahead. It's back through the cooler.

OLD MAN

Thanks son. Say—what kind of toilet paper you got back there?

DANTE

The white kind.

OLD MAN

I'm not asking about the color. I mean is it rough or cottony?

DANTE

Actually, it is kind of rough.

OLD MAN

Rough, eh? Oh, that stuff rips hell out of my hemorrhoids. Say, would you mind if I took a roll of the soft stuff back there. I see you sell the soft stuff.

DANTE

Yeah, but . . .

OLD MAN

Aw, c'mon boy. What's the difference? You said yourself the stuff that's there now is rough.

DANTE

Yeah, okay. Go ahead.

OLD MAN

Thanks son, you're a lifesaver.

The OLD MAN *walks off.* DANTE *heads back to the counter. The* OLD MAN *returns.*

OLD MAN

Say, young fella; you know I hate to bother you again, but can I take a paper or something back there . . . to read? It usually takes me a while, and I like to read while it's going on.

DANTE

Jesus . . . go ahead.

OLD MAN

Thanks, young man. You've got a heart of gold.

The OLD MAN *sifts through some papers and a few magazines. He comes back to the counter.*

DANTE

You know, you probably could've been home, already, in the time it's taken you to get in there.

OLD MAN

Can I trouble you for one of those magazines?

DANTE

I said go ahead.

OLD MAN

No, I mean the ones there. Behind the counter.

DANTE *glances over and reacts.*

DANTE

The porno mags?

OLD MAN

Yeah. I like the cartoons. They make me laugh. They draw the biggest titties.

DANTE

(hands one to him)

Here. Now leave me alone.

OLD MAN

Uh, can I have the other one. The one below this one. They show more in that one.

DANTE *makes the switch.*

OLD MAN

Thanks son. I appreciate this.

The OLD MAN *walks off. We hear the back door open and close, then the*
front door does the same. RANDAL *joins* DANTE.

RANDAL

Helluva game!

DANTE

One ball!! They come all the way here . . . I close the damn store
. . . for one ball!

RANDAL

Hockey's hockey. At least we got to play.

DANTE

Randal, twelve minutes is not a game! Jesus, it's barely a warm-
up!

RANDAL

Bitch, bitch, bitch. You want something to drink?
(walking away)

DANTE

Gatorade.

Pause. Then . . .

(OC) RANDAL

What happened to all the Gatorade?

DANTE

Exactly. They drank it all.

(OC) RANDAL

After an exhausting game like that I can believe it.

DANTE
(as RANDAL*)*
''It's not like we're gonna sell out.''

RANDAL *comes back with drinks.*

RANDAL

You know what Sanford told me?
(offering drink)

DANTE

I still can't believe Caitlin's getting married.

RANDAL

Julie Dwyer died.

DANTE

Yeah, right.

RANDAL

No, I'm serious.

DANTE *is visibly taken aback.*

DANTE

Oh, my god.

RANDAL

Sanford's brother dates her cousin. He found out this morning.

DANTE

How? When?

RANDAL

Embolism in her brain. Yesterday.

DANTE

Jesus.

RANDAL

She was swimming at the YMCA pool when it happened. Died midbackstroke.

DANTE

I haven't seen her in almost two years.

RANDAL

Correct me if I'm wrong, but wasn't she one of the illustrious twelve?

                    DANTE

Number six.

                    RANDAL

You've had sex with a dead person.

                    DANTE

I'm gonna go to her wake.

                    RANDAL

No, you're not.

                    DANTE

Why not?

                    RANDAL

It's today.

                    DANTE

What!?

                    RANDAL

Paulsen's Funeral Parlor. The next show is at four.

                    DANTE

Shit. What about tomorrow?

                    RANDAL

One night only. She's buried in the morning.

                    DANTE

You've gotta watch the store. I have to go to this.

                    RANDAL

Wait, wait, wait. Has it occurred to you that I might be bereaved
as well?

                    DANTE

You hardly knew her!

                    RANDAL

True, but do you know how many people are going to be there?
All of our old classmates, to say the least.

DANTE

Stop it. This is beneath even you.

RANDAL

I'm not missing what's probably going to be the social event of the season.

DANTE

You hate people.

RANDAL

But I love gatherings. Isn't it ironic?

DANTE

Don't be an asshole. Somebody has to stay with the store.

RANDAL

If you go, I go.

DANTE

She meant nothing to you!

RANDAL

She meant nothing to you either until I told you she died.

DANTE

I'm not taking you to this funeral.

RANDAL

I'm going with you.

DANTE

I can't close the store.

RANDAL

You just closed the store to play hockey on the roof!

DANTE

Exactly, which means I can't close it for another hour so we can both go to a wake.

Cut to:

INT CAR: DAY

DANTE *drives with passenger* RANDAL, their backs to the camera.

> RANDAL
> You were saying?

> DANTE
> Thanks for putting me in a tough spot. You're a good friend.

Silence. Then . . .

> RANDAL
> She was pretty young, hunhh?

> DANTE
> Twenty-two; same as us.

> RANDAL
> An embolism in a pool.

> DANTE
> An embarrassing way to die.

> RANDAL
> That's nothing compared to how my cousin Walter died.

> DANTE
> How'd he die?

> RANDAL
> Broke his neck.

> DANTE
> That's embarrassing?

> RANDAL
> He broke his neck trying to suck his own dick.

Absolute silence. Then . . .

DANTE

Shut the hell up.

RANDAL

Bible truth.

DANTE

Stop it.

RANDAL

I swear.

DANTE

Oh, my god.

RANDAL

Come on. Haven't you ever tried to suck your own dick?

DANTE

No!

RANDAL

Yeah sure. You're so repressed.

DANTE

Because I never tried to suck my own dick?

RANDAL

No, because you won't admit to it. As if a guy's a fucking pervert because he tries to go down on himself. You're as curious as the rest of us, pal. You've tried it.

DANTE

Who found him?

RANDAL

My cousin? My aunt found him. On his bed, doubled over himself with his legs on top. Dick in his mouth. My aunt freaked out. It was a mess.

DANTE

His dick was in his mouth?

                                    RANDAL
           Balls resting on his lips.

                                    DANTE
           He made it, hunhh?

                                    RANDAL
           Yeah, but at what a price.

Silence. Then . . .

                                    DANTE
           I could never reach.

                                    RANDAL
           Reach what?

                                    DANTE
           You know.

                                    RANDAL
           What, your dick?

                                    DANTE
           Yeah. Like you said, you know. I guess everyone tries it, sooner
           or later.

                                    RANDAL
           I never tried it.

DANTE *glares at* RANDAL. *Silence. Then . . .*

           Fucking pervert.

Cut to:

EXT: FUNERAL PARLOR. DAY

DANTE *and* RANDAL *walk up the path to the funeral parlor.*

                                    DANTE
           I know it was a bad idea to close the store.

RANDAL

Listen to you.

DANTE

I can't help it. At least when we were playing hockey outside, I could see if anyone wanted to go in.

RANDAL

Nobody's there. It's four o'clock on a Saturday. How many people ever come to the store at four on a Saturday?

Cut to:

EXT: CONVENIENCE STORE. DAY

A MASSIVE CROWD *is outside the store. Cut to:*

EXT: FUNERAL PARLOR. DAY

DANTE *and* RANDAL *run from the front door, closely chased by a small crowd of angry mourners. Car locks are slammed down. The car screams away. The pursuing crowd stands in the middle of the street, shaking their fists, throwing things. Cut to:*

EXT: CONVENIENCE STORE. NIGHT

The car pulls up and RANDAL *and* DANTE *get out. Absolutely nobody is outside.*

DANTE
(furious)

I can't fucking believe you!!

RANDAL

I'm telling you, it wasn't my fault!

DANTE

You knocked the fucking casket over, for Chrissakes!

RANDAL

I was just leaning on it! It was an accident!

DANTE

Does anyone ever knock over a casket on purpose?

                              RANDAL

So the casket fell over! Big deal!

                              DANTE

Her fucking body fell out!

                              RANDAL

So they'll put her back in! It's not like it's gonna matter if she
breaks something!

                              DANTE
                          (opening door)
Just . . . go! Go open the video store.

                           (OC) JAY
                          (mimicking)
Yeah! Open the video store!!

                              RANDAL
                           (to OC)
Shut the fuck up, junkie!

JAY *enters the frame, right next to* RANDAL. *He aims his butt at him and
farts.* RANDAL *lunges for him.* DANTE *grabs* RANDAL.

                              DANTE
                         (to RANDAL)
Go open the video store.

                               JAY

Yeah, you cock-smoking clerk.

                              DANTE
                           (to JAY)
How many times I gotta tell you not to deal outside the store.

                               JAY

I'm not dealing.

A KID *tugs at* JAY'S *shirt.*

                               KID

You got anything, man?

Yeah, what do you want?

RANDAL *heads to the video store.* DANTE *enters the convenience store and slides the sign to* OPEN. *After a few seconds, the* IMPATIENT CUSTOMER *(guy who lost his keys) appears, flashlight in hand, scanning the ground.*

IMPATIENT CUSTOMER
(to JAY*)*
Hey, did you see a set of keys lying around here somewhere?

Cut to:

INT: CONVENIENCE STORE. NIGHT

DANTE *rearranges the milk.* RANDAL *joins him.*

RANDAL
Let me borrow your car.

DANTE
I don't want to talk to you.

RANDAL
Fine. Just lend me your car.

DANTE
Why should I loan you my car?

RANDAL
I want to rent a movie.

DANTE
(pause)
You want to rent a movie.

RANDAL
I want to rent a movie.

DANTE *walks away, shaking his head.*

RANDAL
What's that for?

DANTE

You work in a video store!

They head back to the counter.

RANDAL

I work in a shitty video store. I want to go to a good video store so I can rent a good movie.

CUSTOMER

Are you open?

DANTE *and* RANDAL
(simultaneously)

YES!

The CUSTOMER *comes to the counter.*

CUSTOMER

Pack of cigarettes.
(pets cat)
Cute cat. What's its name?

RANDAL

Annoying Customer.

The CUSTOMER *lets it sink in, and then leaves in a huff.* DANTE *puts up cigarettes.*

DANTE

Can you imagine being halfway decent to the customers at least some of the time?

RANDAL

Let me borrow your car.

DANTE
(calmer)

May I be blunt with you?

RANDAL

If you must.

DANTE

We are employees of Quick Stop Convenience and RST video, respectively. As such, we have certain responsibilities which—though it may seem cruel and unusual—does include manning our posts until closing.

RANDAL

I see. So playing hockey and attending wakes—these practices are standard operating procedure.

DANTE

There's a difference. Those were obligations. Obligations that could not have been met at any later date. Now renting videos—that's just gratuitous, not to mention illogical, considering you work in a video store.

Another CUSTOMER *leans in.*

CUSTOMER

Are you open?

DANTE
(rolls his eyes)

Yes.

RANDAL

You know what? I don't think I care for your rationale.

DANTE

It's going to have to do for now, considering that it's my car that's up for request.

(to CUSTOMER*)*

Can I help you?

CUSTOMER

Pack of cigarettes.

RANDAL

What's your point?

DANTE

My point is that you're a clerk, paid to do a job. You can't just do anything you want while you're working.

CUSTOMER
(reading tabloid)
"Space Alien Revealed as Head of Time Warner; Reports Stock Increase."

(to DANTE and RANDAL)

They print any kind of shit in these papers.

DANTE

They certainly do. Two fifty-five.

RANDAL

So your argument is that title dictates behavior?

DANTE

What?

RANDAL

The reason you won't let me borrow your car is because I have a title and a job description, and I'm supposed to follow it, right?

DANTE

Exactly.

CUSTOMER
(interjecting)
I saw one, one time, that said the world was ending the next week. Then in the next week's paper, they said we were miraculously saved at the zero hour by a Koala-fish mutant bird. Crazy shit.

RANDAL
(eyes the CUSTOMER, annoyed)
So I'm no more responsible for my own decisions while I'm here at work than, say, the Death Squad soldiers in Bosnia?

DANTE

That's stretching it. You're not being asked to slay children or anything.

RANDAL

Not yet.

(sips water)

CUSTOMER
(again with the interjections)
And I remember this one time the damn paper said . . .

RANDAL *spits a mist of water at the customer, drenching him. The man reacts violently, attempting to grab* RANDAL *from over the counter.* RANDAL *makes no move, but remains untouched.* DANTE *plays block.*

CUSTOMER
I'M GONNA BREAK YOUR FUCKING HEAD! YOU FUCKING JERKOFF!

DANTE
Sir! Sir, I'm sorry! He didn't mean it! He was trying to get me.

CUSTOMER

Well, he missed!

DANTE
I know. I'm sorry. Let me refund your cigarette money, and we'll call it even.

CUSTOMER
(considerably calmer; takes money)
This is the last time I ever come here.
(to RANDAL)
And if I ever see you again, I'm gonna break your fucking head open!

The CUSTOMER *leaves, wiping water from his face.* RANDAL *salutes him.*

DANTE
(angrily)
What the fuck did you do that for?

RANDAL

Two reasons: one, I hate when the people can't shut up about the stupid tabloid headlines.

                              DANTE
Jesus!

                              RANDAL
And two, to make a point: title does not dictate behavior.

                              DANTE
What?

                              RANDAL
If title dictated my behavior, as a clerk serving the public, I
wouldn't be allowed to spit a mouthful of water at that guy. But I
did, so my point is that people dictate their own behavior. Hence,
even though I'm a clerk in this video store, I choose to go rent
videos at Big Choice.
                    (extends opened palm)
Agreed?

                              DANTE
                (shakes his head; hands over keys)
You're a danger to both the dead and the living.

                              RANDAL
I like to think I'm a master of my own destiny.

                              DANTE
Please, get the hell out of here.

                              RANDAL
I know I'm your hero.

RANDAL *exits. Cut to:*

INT: CONVENIENCE STORE. DAY

DANTE *waits on a customer (*TRAINER*). He lifts the gallon of milk into
a paper bag, letting out a slight grunt.*

                              TRAINER
Sounds to me like somebody needs to hit the gym.

                              DANTE
Excuse me?

TRAINER

I heard you strain when you put the milk in the bag. That milk
only weighs about seven pounds.

DANTE

I didn't strain. I sighed.

TRAINER

I don't think so. That was a grunt; a deep inhalation of oxygen to
aid in the stretching of muscles. I'm a trainer. I know what that
sound signifies: you're out of shape.

DANTE

I don't think so.

TRAINER

Oh, I do. You made the same noise when you reached across the
counter for my cash. Your muscles are thin and sadly
underutilized.

DANTE

They are not.

TRAINER

Yes, they are. You're out of shape.

DANTE

What are you talking about? There's no fat on this body.

TRAINER

No fat, but no tone either. You don't get enough exercise.

A female customer (HEATHER) leans in the doorway.

HEATHER

Are you open?

DANTE

Yes.

HEATHER
(grabs a paper)

Just the paper.

DANTE
(to HEATHER*)*

Thirty-five.

TRAINER
(to HEATHER*)*
Let me ask you a question: Do you think this guy's out of shape?

HEATHER
(studies DANTE*)*
I don't know. I can't really tell from here.

TRAINER

He is.

DANTE

I am not.

TRAINER
How much can you bench?

DANTE

I don't know.

HEATHER
(studying DANTE*)*
I'd say about sixty, seventy—tops.

DANTE
I know I can bench more than that!

TRAINER
I think the lady called it.

HEATHER
My ex-boyfriend was about his height, but he was much bulkier.
He could bench two-fifty, three hundred easy.

TRAINER
I do about three-fifty, four.

HEATHER

No way!

                           TRAINER
                      (rolling up sleeve)
Feel that.

                           HEATHER
That's tight. Solid.

                           TRAINER
Now feel his.
                        (to DANTE)
Roll up your sleeve, chief.

                           DANTE
Oh for God's sake!

                           TRAINER
See? You're ashamed. You know you're out of shape. Take my
card. I can help you tone that body up in no time. Get you on an
aerobics and free-weights program.

A SUITED MAN *carrying a notebook comes to the counter.*

                         SUITED MAN
You open?

                           DANTE
                        (to MAN)
Yes.
                      (to TRAINER)
I'm not out of shape.

                         SUITED MAN
Excuse me, but have you been here all day?

                           DANTE
What?

                           HEATHER
                    (still studying DANTE)
He's got those love handles.

                           DANTE
                      (to HEATHER)
I don't have love handles.

SUITED MAN
Were you working here at about four o'clock?

DANTE
I've been here since six o'clock this morning. Why?

TRAINER
(to HEATHER*)*
It's probably from being around all this food every day.

HEATHER
Oh, I know. If I had to work here all day, I'd be bloated and out of shape, too.

DANTE
I'm not out of shape!

SUITED MAN
Can I have your name please?

DANTE
Dante Hicks. Why? What is this about?

The SUITED MAN *scribbles in his notebook.*

HEATHER
You're Dante Hicks? Oh my God! I didn't even recognize you!

TRAINER
Because he's out of shape.

DANTE
Do I know you?

HEATHER
Do you remember Alyssa Jones? She hung out with . . .

DANTE
Caitlin Bree. Yeah?

HEATHER
I'm her sister.

DANTE

You're Alyssa's sister? Heather?

HEATHER

Yep. I remember you got caught in my parents' room with Caitlin
once.

TRAINER

Did you say Caitlin Bree?

DANTE

Yeah.

TRAINER

Pretty girl, about this girl's height—dark hair—gorgeous body?

DANTE

Yeah?

TRAINER

And your name is Dante Hicks? You went to high school with
her? You played hockey?

DANTE

How do you know that?

TRAINER

Oh man! Hey, you still going out with her?

DANTE

No, she's getting married.

TRAINER

To you?

HEATHER

To an Asian design major.

TRAINER

Shit!
(to DANTE)
Don't take this the wrong way, but I used to fuck her.

DANTE

What?

TRAINER

While you two were dating in high school. We're talking four, five years ago, back when I drove a Trans-Am.

HEATHER

Oh my God! You're Rick Derris?

TRAINER

Yeah!

DANTE

You know him?

HEATHER

Caitlin used to talk about him all the time.

TRAINER

Really?

HEATHER

Oh yeah. You were the built older guy with the black Trans and the big . . .

DANTE

Wait a second!
(to TRAINER*)*
You used to sleep with Caitlin Bree? While I was dating her?

TRAINER

All the time. That girl was like a rabbit.

DANTE

I . . . I don't believe this. . . .

HEATHER
(to TRAINER*)*
I still remember Caitlin telling us about that time you two went to that motel—the one with the mirrors and the hot tub in the room.

DANTE

THE GLADES MOTEL?

TRAINER

Holy shit! She told you about that!

(to DANTE*)*

Buddy of mine worked there. Said he watched the whole thing.
They used to film people at that hotel; nobody knew about it.

HEATHER

She said one time you set up a tent on the beach and you guys
did it in the middle of this big rainstorm.

DANTE

What? When? When did all this shit happen?

TRAINER

Hey man, that was a long time ago. Don't let it get to you.

HEATHER

I'm surprised you never found out about it, Dante. Everybody in
school knew—even in my class.

DANTE

Jesus Christ, what next?

The SUITED MAN *rips a piece of paper out of his notebook and hands it
to* DANTE.

SUITED MAN

Here you go.

DANTE

What's this?

SUITED MAN

A fine, for five hundred dollars.

DANTE

WHAT?

TRAINER

Five hundred bucks? What for?

SUITED MAN

For violation of New Jersey Statute Section Two A, number one-
seventy slash fifty-one: Any person who sells or makes available

tobacco or tobacco-related products to persons under the age of eighteen is regarded as disorderly.

DANTE

What are you talking about?

SUITED MAN

According to the NJAC—the New Jersey Administrative Code, section eighteen, five, slash twelve point five—a fine of no less than two hundred and fifty dollars is to be leveled against any person reported selling cigarettes to a minor.

DANTE

I didn't do that!

SUITED MAN

You said you were here all day?

DANTE

Yeah, but I didn't sell cigarettes to any kids!

SUITED MAN

An angry mother called the state division of taxation and complained that the man working at Quick Stop Convenience sold her five-year-old daughter cigarettes today at around four o'clock. Division of taxation calls the State Board of Health, and they send me down here to issue a fine. You say you were working all day, hence the fine is yours. It's doubled due to the incredibly young age of the child.

DANTE

But I didn't sell cigarettes to any kid!

TRAINER

To a five-year-old kid? What a scumbag!

HEATHER

That's sick, Dante.

DANTE

I didn't sell cigarettes to any kids! I swear!

SUITED MAN

The due date is on the bottom. This summons cannot be contested in any court of law. Failure to remit before the due date will result in a charge of criminal negligence, and a warrant will be issued for your arrest. Have a nice day.

The SUITED MAN *exits, with* DANTE *trying to follow.*

DANTE

But I didn't sell cigarettes to any kids! Hey!

TRAINER

(takes back the card)

Forget it. I don't want to deal with a guy that sells cigarettes to a five-year-old.

(to HEATHER*)*

Can I offer you a ride somewhere?

HEATHER

Sure. How about the beach?

TRAINER

I like the way you think.

The two exit. DANTE, *alone, studies his summons. He rubs his forehead.*

DANTE

Jesus! What next?

(OC) VOICE

Dante?

DANTE *spins, angrily.*

DANTE

What?

His expression softens.

Caitlin?

Cut to:

EXT: VIDEO STORE. NIGHT

JAY *deals with a customer as* SILENT BOB *looks on.*

> JAY
>
> That's the price, my brother.

> JOHN
>
> Yo, I don't have that kind of cash.

> JAY
>
> For this kind of hash, you need that kind of cash.

> JOHN
>
> How long you gonna be here?

> JAY
>
> Till ten. Then I'm going to John K's party.

> JOHN
>
> You're gonna be at John K's party?

> JAY
> *(to* SILENT BOB*)*

My man is deaf.
> *(yelling)*
> I'M GOING TO JOHN K'S PARTY!
> *(quieter)*

Neh.

> JOHN
>
> Yo, don't sell all that. 'Cause I'm gonna get the cash and buy it
> from you at John K's. You're gonna bring it, right?

> JAY
>
> The only place I don't bring my drugs is church. And that ain't
> till Sunday morning.

> JOHN
>
> Yo. I'll see you at that party.
> *(puts his hand up to be slapped)*
> I'll see you there?

JAY
(reluctantly slapping hands)
I'll see you there.

JOHN *leaves.* JAY *turns to* SILENT BOB.

JAY
It's motherfuckers like that who give recreational drug users a
bad name.
(suddenly spotting someone OC)
HEY BABY! YOU EVER HAD YOUR ASSHOLE LICKED?

Cut to:

INT: CONVENIENCE STORE. NIGHT

DANTE *and* CAITLIN *are embracing very tightly. We hold on them for a
few seconds, just to let it sink in. Then . . .*

DANTE
When did you get back?

CAITLIN
Just now.

DANTE
My God. I haven't seen you since . . .
(he hugs her again)

CAITLIN
Dante. You've got a customer.

DANTE *hops behind the counter. A customer pays for something while*
DANTE *continues to talk.*

CAITLIN
I just saw Alyssa's little sister outside. She was with Rick Derris.

DANTE
Let's not talk about that. How'd you get home?

CAITLIN
Train. It took eight hours.

                    DANTE
    I can't believe you're here.

Another customer comes to the counter.

                    CUSTOMER
    Excuse me, do you have . . .

                    DANTE
                  (to CUSTOMER)
    To the back, above the oil.
                  (to CAITLIN)
    How long are you staying?

                    CAITLIN
    Until Monday. Then I have to take the train back.

Yet another customer comes to the counter.

                    CUSTOMER
    Pack of cigarettes.
                  (to CAITLIN)
    Congratulations. I saw that announcement in today's paper.
                  (to DANTE)
    She's marrying an Asian design major.

                    DANTE
    So I'm told.

Cut to:

EXT: VIDEO STORE. NIGHT

JAY *and* SILENT BOB *lean against the wall.*

                    JAY
    Man, it's fucking slow.

SILENT BOB *walks out of the frame, leaving* JAY *alone against the wall. He comes back a few seconds later, carrying a mini-Walkman with ten-watt speakers. He sets it down on the ground and turns it on. House music starts playing. Jay—possessed by the beat—breaks into an impromptu*

dance, in which he makes suggestive and often lewd moves. SILENT BOB
leans against the wall. Cut to:

INT: VIDEO STORE. NIGHT

On counter

> CAITLIN
>
> You're just going to lock the store like that?

> DANTE
>
> I want to talk to you about something, and I don't want to be
> disturbed.

> CAITLIN
>
> You saw it?

> DANTE
>
> Very dramatic, I thought.

> CAITLIN
>
> It's not what you think.

> DANTE
>
> What, it's worse? You're pregnant with an Asian design major's
> child?

> CAITLIN
>
> I'm not pregnant.

> DANTE
>
> Were you going to tell me or just send me an invitation?

> CAITLIN
>
> I was going to tell you. But then we were getting along so well, I
> didn't want to mess it up.

> DANTE
>
> You could've broke it to me gently, you know; at least started by
> telling me you had a boyfriend. I told you I had a girlfriend.

> CAITLIN
>
> I know, I'm sorry. But when we started talking . . . it's like I
> forgot I had a boyfriend. And then he proposed last month. . . .

DANTE

And you said yes?

CAITLIN

Well . . . kind of, sort of?

DANTE

Is that what they teach you at that school of yours? Kind of, sort of? Everyone knows about this except me! Do you know how humiliating that is?

CAITLIN

I would've told you, and you would have stopped calling, like a baby.

DANTE

How do you know that?

CAITLIN

Because I know you. You prefer drastic measures to rational ones.

DANTE

So you're really getting married?

CAITLIN

No.

DANTE

No, you're not really getting married?

CAITLIN

The story goes like this: He proposed, and I told him I had to think about it, and he insisted I wear the ring anyway. Then my mother told the paper we were engaged.

DANTE

How like her.

CAITLIN

Then my mother called me this morning and told me the announcement was in the paper. That's when I hopped the train to come back here, because I knew you'd be a wreck.

DANTE

Thanks for the vote of confidence.

CAITLIN

Was I right?

DANTE

Wreck is a harsh term. Disturbed is more like it. Mildly disturbed even.

CAITLIN

I love a macho facade. It's such a turn-on.
(sniffing air)
What smells like shoe polish?

DANTE

And you came here to what? To comfort me?

CAITLIN

The last thing I needed was for you to think I was hiding something from you.

DANTE

But you were.

CAITLIN

No, I wasn't. Not really. I told you'd I'd been seeing other people.

DANTE

Yeah, but not seriously. Christ, you're ready to walk down the aisle—I'd say that constitutes something more than just seeing somebody.

CAITLIN

I'm giving him his ring back.

DANTE

What?

CAITLIN

I don't want to marry him. I don't want to get married now. I'm on the verge of graduation. I want to go to grad school after this. And then I want to start a career. I don't want to be a wife first, and then have to worry about when I'm going to fit in all of the other stuff. I've come way too far and studied too hard to let my education go to waste as a housewife. And I know that's what I'd become. Sang's already signed with a major firm, and he's going to be pulling a huge salary, which would give me no reason to work, and he's so traditional anyway . . .

DANTE

Sang? His name is a past tense?

CAITLIN

Stop it. He's a nice guy.

DANTE

If he's so nice, why aren't you going to marry him?

CAITLIN

I just told you.

DANTE

There's more, isn't there?

CAITLIN

Why, Mr. Hicks—whatever do you mean?

DANTE

Tell me I don't have something to do with it.

CAITLIN

You don't have anything to do with it.

DANTE

You lie.

CAITLIN

Look how full of yourself you are.

DANTE

I just believe in giving credit where credit is due. And I believe that I'm the impetus behind your failure to wed.

CAITLIN

If I'm so nuts about you, then why am I having sex with an Asian design major?

DANTE

Jesus, you're caustic.

CAITLIN

I had to bring you down from that cloud you were floating on.
When I say I don't want to get married, I mean just that. I don't
want to marry anybody. Not for years.

DANTE

So who's asking? I don't want to marry you.

CAITLIN

Good. Stay in that frame of mind.

DANTE

But can we date?

CAITLIN

I'm sure Sang and—Veronica?—would like that.

DANTE

We could introduce them. They might hit it off.

CAITLIN

You're serious. You want to date again.

DANTE

I would like to be your boyfriend, yes.

CAITLIN

It's just the shock of seeing me after three years. Believe me,
you'll get over it.

DANTE

Give me a bit more credit. I think it's time we got back together,
you know. I'm more mature, you're more mature, you're finishing
college, I'm already in the job market . . .

CAITLIN

You work in a market, all right.

DANTE

Cute. Tell me you wouldn't want to go out again. After all the
talking we've been doing.

CAITLIN

The key word here is *talk,* Dante. I think the idea, the conception of us dating is more idyllic than what actually happens when we date.

DANTE

So . . . what? So we should just make pretend over the phone that we're dating?

CAITLIN

I don't know. Maybe we should just see what happens.

DANTE

Let me take you out tonight.

CAITLIN

You mean, on a date?

DANTE

Yes. A real date. Dinner and a movie.

CAITLIN

The Dante Hicks Dinner and a Movie Date. I think I've been on that one before.

DANTE

You have a better suggestion?

CAITLIN

How about the Caitlin Bree Walk on the Boardwalk, Then Get Naked Somewhere Kind of Private Date?

DANTE

I hear that's a rather popular date.

CAITLIN
(hits him)
Jerk. Here I am, throwing myself at you, succumbing to your wily charms, and you call me a slut, in so many words.

DANTE

What about Sing?

CAITLIN

Sang.

DANTE

Sang.

CAITLIN

He's not invited.

DANTE

He's your fiancé.

CAITLIN

I offer you my body and you offer me semantics? He's just a boyfriend, Dante, and in case you haven't gotten the drift of why I came all the way here from Ohio, I'm about to become single again. And yes—let me placate your ego—you are the inspiration for this bold and momentous decision, for which I'll probably be ostracized at both school and home. You ask me who I choose, I choose you.

DANTE

So what are you saying?

CAITLIN

You're such an asshole.

DANTE

I'm just kidding.

CAITLIN

I can already tell this isn't going to work.

DANTE

I'll ask Randal to close up for me—when he gets back.

CAITLIN

Where'd he go? I'd have thought he'd be at your side, like an obedient lapdog.

DANTE

He went to rent a movie, but he hasn't gotten back yet. Ah, screw it; I'll just lock the store up and leave him a note.

CAITLIN

You're too responsible. But no. I have to go home first. They don't
even know I left school. And I should break the disengagement
news to my mother, which is going to cause quite a row,
considering she loves Sang.

DANTE

Who doesn't?

CAITLIN

Well, me I guess.
                        (gathering herself to go)
So, I shall take my leave of you, but I will return in a little while,
at which time—yes—I would love to go for dinner and a movie
with you.

DANTE

What happened to the walk and the nakedness?

CAITLIN

I'm easy, but I'm not that easy.
                        (she kisses his cheek)
See you later, handsome.

DANTE *watches her leave. He then explodes in jubilance.*

DANTE

YES!

Cut to:

INT: CONVENIENCE STORE. NIGHT

DANTE *looks ahead, dreamily, half-spinning in his chair.* RANDAL
enters carrying videos.

RANDAL

Get to work.

DANTE
                        (takes videos)
What'd you rent?
                        (reads)
Best of Both Worlds?

RANDAL

Hermaphroditic porn. Starlets with both organs. You should see
the box: Beautiful women with dicks that put mine to shame.

DANTE

And this is what you rented?

RANDAL

I like to expand my horizons.

DANTE

I got fined for selling cigarettes to a minor.

RANDAL

No way!

DANTE

Five hundred dollars.

RANDAL

You're bullshitting.

DANTE *hands him the summons.* RANDAL *reads it.*

RANDAL

I didn't think they even enforced this.

DANTE
(points to himself)

Living proof.

RANDAL

I thought you never sold cigarettes to kids.

DANTE

I don't; you did.

RANDAL
(pause)

Really?

DANTE

Little girl. Maybe five years old?

RANDAL
(taken aback)

Holy shit. That girl?

DANTE

As opposed to the hundreds of other children you let buy
cigarettes whenever you work here.

RANDAL

Then how come you got the fine?

DANTE

Because I'm here.

RANDAL
(incredulous)

You're lying.

DANTE

I swear. I couldn't make this kind of hell up.

RANDAL

Then why aren't you like screaming at me right now?

DANTE

Because I'm happy.

RANDAL

You're happy?

DANTE

I'm happy.

RANDAL

You're happy to get a fine?

DANTE

No, I'm happy because Caitlin came to see me.

RANDAL

Now I know you're lying.

DANTE

I'm not. She just left.

                    RANDAL

What did she say?

                    DANTE

She's not going to marry that guy. She went home to tell her
mother.

                    RANDAL

You're kidding.

                    DANTE

I'm not.

                    RANDAL
              (takes it in for a moment)
Wow. You've had quite an evening.

                    DANTE

She went home, she's getting ready, and we're going out.

                    RANDAL

I feel so ineffectual. Is there anything I can do for you?

                    DANTE

Watch the store while I go home and change.

                    RANDAL

What happened to title dictates behavior?

                    DANTE

This is my way of spitting water at life.

                    RANDAL
              (suddenly aware)
Hey, what about Veronica?

                    DANTE

No! Don't bring it up. I don't want to think about that now. Let
me enjoy this hour of bliss. I'll think about all of that later. In the
meantime, nobody mentions the *V* word.

                    RANDAL

You're a snake.

DANTE

In my absence, try not to sell cigarettes to any newborns.

RANDAL

You want me to bring the VCR over here so we can watch this?

DANTE

I might be leaving early to go out with Caitlin, in which case you'll have to close the store tonight.

RANDAL

All right, but you're missing out. Chicks with dicks.

DANTE

(puts cat on counter)

I'll read the book.

DANTE *exits. A* CUSTOMER *comes back to the counter. He pets the cat.*

CUSTOMER

Cute cat. What's his name.

RANDAL

Peptic ulcer.

Cut to:

EXT: CONVENIENCE STORE. NIGHT

JAY *and* SILENT BOB *watch as* DANTE *passes. A small group of burners are poised around the store door.* JAY *carefully writes on a large piece of paper, using a thick marker.* SILENT BOB *hands him the scissors.* JAY *slowly cuts the large piece of paper.* SILENT BOB *hands him the tape.* JAY *snaps off a few pieces, and plasters the sign to the convenience store door. It is a large word balloon, and it reads* I EAT COCK! *Once in place, he raps on the window.* RANDAL *looks out, his face adjacent to the word balloon, making it appear as if he is saying he eats cock. The small group laughs hysterically. Cut to:*

INT: CONVENIENCE STORE. NIGHT

CAITLIN *enters, carrying an overnight bag.* RANDAL *is watching his porno. The porno is loud and lewd.* CAITLIN *stares.*

CAITLIN

Randal Graves—scourge of the video renter.

RANDAL

Ladies and gentlemen, Mrs. Asian Design Major herself: Caitlin
Bree!

CAITLIN

You saw that article? God, isn't it awful? My mother sent that in.

RANDAL

I take it she likes the guy.

CAITLIN

You'd think she was marrying him. What are you watching?

RANDAL

Children's programming. What did your mom say when you told
her you weren't engaged anymore?

CAITLIN

She said not to come home until graduation.

RANDAL

Wow, you got thrown out? For Dante?

CAITLIN

What can I say? He does weird things to me.

RANDAL

Can I watch?

CAITLIN

You can hold me down.

RANDAL

Can I join in?

CAITLIN

You might be let down. I'm not a hermaphrodite.

RANDAL

Few are. So what makes you think you can maintain a relationship
with Dante this time around?

CAITLIN

A woman's intuition. Something in me says it's time to give the old boy a serious try.

RANDAL

Wow. Hey, I was just about to order some dinner. You eat Chinese, right?

CAITLIN

Dick.

RANDAL

Exactly.

CAITLAN

So where is he?

RANDAL

He went home to change for the big date.

CAITLIN

God, isn't he great?

RANDAL
(indicating TV)

No, *this* is great.

CAITLIN

Can I use the bathroom?

RANDAL

There's no light back there.

CAITLIN

Why aren't there any lights?

RANDAL

Well, there are, but for some reason they stop working at five-fourteen every night.

CAITLIN

You're kidding.

RANDAL

Nobody can figure it out. And the boss doesn't want to pay the electrician to fix it, because the electrician owes money to the video store.

CAITLIN

Such a sordid state of affairs.

RANDAL

And I'm caught in the middle—torn between my loyalty for the boss, and my desire to piss with the light on.

CAITLIN

I'll try to manage.

She heads toward the back.

RANDAL

Hey Caitlin . . .
(cautionary)
Break his heart again this time, and I'll kill you. Nothing personal.

CAITLIN

You're very protective of him, Randal. You always have been.

RANDAL

Territoriality. He was mine first.

CAITLIN
(rubs his head)
Awww. That was so cute.

She kisses his forehead and walks away. The MOTHER *and* SMALL CHILD (Happy Scrappy) *come to the counter.*

MOTHER
(oblivious of the TV)
A pack of cigarettes.

The SMALL CHILD *points at the TV screen.*

SMALL CHILD

Cunt!

Cut to:

INT: CONVENIENCE STORE. NIGHT

RANDAL *studies the* I EAT COCK *word balloon.* DANTE *enters.*

DANTE

Who eats cock?

RANDAL

Bunch of savages in this town.
  (recalling)
Hey, Caitlin's in the back. You might want to see if she's okay;
she's been back there a long time.

DANTE

There's no lights back there.

RANDAL

I told her that. She said she didn't need any. Why don't you join
her, man. Make a little bathroom bam-bam.

DANTE

I love your sexy talk. It's so . . . kindergarten: Poo-poo; wee-wee.

RANDAL

Fuck you.

The cooler door is heard opening. CAITLIN *walks lazily down the*
convenience store aisle. She looks very satisfied. DANTE *and* RANDAL
regard her curiously. She joins them, latching on to DANTE's *arm,*
lovingly.

CAITLIN

How'd you get here so fast?

DANTE

I left like an hour ago.

CAITLIN
(regards him curiously)
Do you always talk weird after you violate women?

RANDAL *and* DANTE *stare at* CAITLIN, *confused.*

RANDAL
Maybe the Asian design major slipped her some opium?

DANTE
Could be.

CAITLIN
(hugging DANTE)
Promise me it'll always be like that.

DANTE
Like what?

CAITLIN
When you just lie perfectly still and let me do everything.

DANTE
Um . . . okay.

RANDAL
Am I missing something here?

CAITLIN
I went back there, and Dante was already waiting for me.

RANDAL
He was?

CAITLIN
It was so cool. He didn't say a word. He was just . . . ready, you
know? And we didn't kiss or talk or anything. He just sat there
and let me do all the work.

RANDAL
(to DANTE)
You dog! I didn't see you go back there.

DANTE *is bewildered.*

CAITLIN

And the fact that there weren't any lights made it so . . .
(she lets out a growl and hugs DANTE*)*
God! That was so great!

DANTE
(quietly)

It wasn't me.

CAITLIN
(laughing it off)
Yeah, right. Who was it: Randal?

DANTE
(to RANDAL*)*

Was it you?

RANDAL

I was up here the whole time.

CAITLIN
(half-laughing)
You two better quit it.

DANTE

I'm serious.

CAITLIN
(beat)
We didn't just have sex in the bathroom?

DANTE

No.

Everyone is silent. Then . . .

CAITLIN

Stop this. This isn't funny.

DANTE
I'm not kidding. I just got back from outside.

CAITLIN
(covering her chest)
This isn't fucking funny, Dante!

DANTE
I'm not fooling around!
(to RANDAL)
Who went back there?

RANDAL
Nobody! I swear!

CAITLIN
I feel nauseous.

DANTE
Are you sure somebody was back there?

CAITLIN
(hits DANTE)
I didn't just fuck myself! Jesus, I'm going to be sick!

RANDAL
You just fucked a total stranger?

DANTE
Shut the fuck up!

CAITLIN
I can't believe this! I feel faint . . .

DANTE
(to RANDAL)
Call the police.

RANDAL
Why?

CAITLIN
No, don't!

DANTE
There's a strange man in our bathroom, and he just raped Caitlin!

CAITLIN
(weakly)

Oh God . . .

RANDAL

She said she did all the work.

DANTE

WOULD YOU SHUT THE FUCK UP?
(pause)
WHO THE FUCK IS IN THE BATHROOM?

Cut to:

INT: COVENIENCE STORE. LATER

THE OLD MAN'S FACE *is serene, almost happy, as he lies on a stretcher. (Same* OLD MAN *who took a porn mag to the bathroom.)*

(OC) CORONER

Who is he?

The body bag zipper is pulled closed. DANTE, *the* CORONER, *and* RANDAL *stand around the stretcher-bound body bag. The* CORONER *takes notes.*

DANTE

I don't know. He just came in and asked to use the bathroom.

CORONER

What time was this?

DANTE

Um . . . I don't know
(to RANDAL*)*
What time did hockey end?

RANDAL

Around three or something.

DANTE

What time did we go to the funeral?

                            RANDAL
I think four.

                            CORONER
Wait a second? Who was working here today?

                            DANTE
Just me.

                            CORONER
I thought you just said you played hockey and went to a funeral.

                            DANTE
We did.

                            CORONER
Then who operated the store?

                            DANTE
Nobody. It was closed.

                            CORONER
With this guy locked in?

                            DANTE
Everything happened at once. I guess I forgot he was back there.

Ambulance attendants join them.

                          ATTENDANT 1
Can we take this now?

                            CORONER
Go ahead.

*The stretcher is wheeled out. Midway down the body bag, something
protrudes, pushing the bag up. It is an erection. RANDAL stares at it.*

                            DANTE
Was he alive when . . . Caitlin . . .

                            CORONER
No. I place the time of death at about three-twenty.

RANDAL

Then how could she . . . you know . . .

CORONER

The body can maintain an erection after expiration. Sometimes
for hours. Did he have the adult magazine when he came in?

DANTE

No. I gave it to him.

RANDAL *and the* CORONER *stare in disbelief.*

DANTE

Well he asked me for it!

CORONER
(continuing)

I can't say for certain until we get him back to the lab, but my
guess is he was masturbating, his heart seized and he died. That's
when the girl found him.
(sniffing the air)
Something smells like shoe polish.

RANDAL
(to CORONER)

This has gotta be the weirdest thing you've ever been called in
on.

CORONER
(writing)

Actually, I once had to tag a kid that broke his neck trying to put
his mouth on his penis.

RANDAL *looks down, anonymously.*

DANTE

What about Caitlin?

CORONER

Shock trauma. She's going to need years of therapy after this. My
question is, How did she come to have sex with the dead man?

DANTE

She thought it was me.

The CORONER *stares at* DANTE.

CORONER

What kind of convenience store do you run here?

He exits. DANTE *and* RANDAL *stare at the floor.*

RANDAL
(beat)
Do you think he was talking about my cousin?

Cut to:

EXT: VIDEO STORE. NIGHT

CAITLIN *sits in the back of the ambulance, a blanket draped over her
shoulders. An attendant takes her blood pressure. The doors are closed
and the vehicle speeds away.* JAY *and* SILENT BOB *lean against the
wall.* JAY *eats sugar out of a box.*

JAY

I knew one of those motherfuckers was gonna kill somebody one
day.

Cut to:

INT: CONVENIENCE STORE. NIGHT

*A jar of salsa is invaded by a large corn chip. Once in the condiment, the
corn chip resembles a surfacing shark fin. Fingers poke at it, bringing it
to life—swimming menacingly to and fro across the jar.*

(OC) RANDAL
(mumbling Jaws *theme)*
Da-dum! Da-dum! Da-dum! DA-DUM! DA-DUM! DA-DUM!

DANTE *and* RANDAL *are on a freezer case.* RANDAL *pushes this chip
around the jar of salsa.* DANTE *stares up at the ceiling, oblivious.*

RANDAL

Salsa shark.

DANTE *says nothing.*

RANDAL
(as Brody)
''We're gonna need a bigger boat.''

DANTE *says even less than nothing.*

RANDAL
(as Quint)
''Man goes into the cage; cage goes into the salsa; shark's in the salsa; our shark.''

DANTE . . . *you know.*

RANDAL
(angry)
What? What's with you? You haven't said anything for like twenty minutes. What the hell is your problem?

DANTE

This life.

RANDAL

This life?

DANTE

Why do I have this life?

RANDAL

Have some chips; you'll feel better.

DANTE

I'm stuck in this pit, earning less than slave wages, working on my day off, dealing with every backward fuck on the planet, the goddam steel shutters are locked all day, I smell like shoe polish, I've got an ex-girlfriend who's catatonic after fucking a dead guy, and my present girlfriend has sucked thirty-six dicks.

RANDAL

Thirty-seven.

DANTE

My life is in the shitter right about now, so if you don't mind, I'd like to stew a bit.

(OC) CUSTOMER

You open?

RANDAL

Yeah.

RANDAL *hops off the freezer case and steps* OC.

(OC) RANDAL

That's all bullshit. You know what the real problem here is?

DANTE

I was born.

RANDAL *comes back.*

RANDAL

You should shit or get off the pot.

DANTE

I should shit or get off the pot.

RANDAL

Yeah, you should shit or get off the pot.

DANTE

What are you talking about?

RANDAL

I'm talking about this thing you have . . . this inability to improve your situation in life.

DANTE

Fuck you.

RANDAL

It's true. You'll sit there and blame life for dealing a cruddy hand, never once accepting the responsibility for the way your situation is.

DANTE

What responsibility?

RANDAL

All right, if you hate this job and the people, and the fact that you have to come in on your day off, then quit.

DANTE

As if it's that easy.

RANDAL

It is. You just up and quit. There are other jobs, and they pay better money. You're bound to be qualified for at least one of them. So what's stopping you?

DANTE

Leave me alone.

RANDAL

You're comfortable. This is a life of convenience for you, and any attempt to change it would shatter the pathetic microcosm you've fashioned for yourself.

DANTE

Oh, like your life's any better?

RANDAL

I'm satisfied with my situation for now. You don't hear me bitching. You, on the other hand, have been bitching all day.

DANTE

Thank you. Why don't you go back to the video store?

RANDAL

It's the same thing with Veronica.

DANTE

Leave her out of this.

RANDAL

You date Veronica because she's low maintenance and because it's convenient. Meanwhile, all you ever do is talk about Caitlin.

You carry a torch for a girl you dated in high school—in high school for God's sake! You're twenty-two!

DANTE

Leave me alone.

RANDAL

If you want Caitlin, then face Veronica, tell her, and be with Caitlin. It you want Veronica, be with Veronica. But don't pine for one and fuck the other. Man, if you weren't such a fucking coward . . .

DANTE

. . . If I wasn't such a fucking coward.
(chuckles)
It must be so great to be able to simplify everything the way you do.

RANDAL

Am I right or what?

DANTE

You're wrong. Things happened today, okay? Things that probably ruined my chances with Caitlin.

RANDAL

What? The dead guy? She'll get over fucking the dead guy. Shit, my mom's been fucking a dead guy for thirty years; I call him Dad.

DANTE

Caitlin and I can't be together. It's impossible.

RANDAL

Melodrama coming from you seems about as natural as an oral bowel movement.

DANTE

What do you want me to say? Yes, I suppose some of the things you're saying may be true. But that's the way things are; it's not going to change.

RANDAL

Make them change.

DANTE

I can't, all right! Jesus, would you leave me alone? I can't make
changes like that in my life. If I could, I would—but I don't have
the ability to risk comfortable situations on the big money and the
fabulous prizes.

RANDAL

Who're you kidding? You can so.

DANTE

Jesus H. Christ, I can't!

RANDAL

So you'll continue being miserable all the time, just because you
don't have the guts to face change?

DANTE
(sadly)
My mother told me once that when I was three, my potty lid was
closed, and instead of lifting it, I chose to shit my pants.

RANDAL

Lovely story.

DANTE

Point is—I'm not the kind of person that disrupts things in order
to shit comfortably.

DANTE *crosses OC. RANDAL* *appears contemplative. Cut to:*

INT: CONVENIENCE STORE. NIGHT

DANTE *repairs ripped dollar bills, taping them back together.* JAY *enters
with* SILENT BOB *and claps his hands.*

JAY
(singing)
Noinch, noinch, noinch—smoking weed, smoking weed! Doing
coke! Drinking beers!
(to DANTE)
A pack of wraps, my good man. It's time to kick back, drink some
beers, and smoke some weed!

DANTE

Done poisoning the youth for the day?

JAY

Hell yes, whatever that means. Now I'm gonna head over to
Atlantic, drink some beers, get ripped, and—please God—get
laid.
                    (pulls out money)
E-Z Wider, one-and-a-halfs.

DANTE

One seventy-nine.

JAY
(to SILENT BOB)
Pay the good man.
                    (to DANTE)
Don't you close soon?

DANTE

A half hour.

JAY

We get off about the same time every night. We should hang out.
You get high?

DANTE

I should start.

JAY

Wanna come to this party tonight? There's gonna be some pussy
there, man!

DANTE

With you? I don't think so.

JAY

Listen to you. Oh shit. "Oh, I don't hang out with drug dealers."

DANTE

Nothing personal.

SILENT BOB *hands weed to* JAY.

JAY

I work, just like you. You're more of a crook than I am, dude.

DANTE

How do you figure . . . HEY! You can't roll a joint in here!

JAY

(rolling a joint)

Relax brother. What I mean is that you sell the stuff in this store at the highest price around. A dollar seventy-nine for wraps— what's that shit?

DANTE

It's not my store.

JAY

And these aren't my drugs—I just sell them.

DANTE

The difference is you exploit a weakness.

JAY

What's that mean?

DANTE

You sell to people that can't stay away from an addiction.

JAY

All right. How much is Pepsi here?

DANTE

A dollar sixty-nine, plus tax.

JAY

At Food City it's ninety-nine cents, plus tax.

DANTE

So.

JAY

So why do you sell it for so much more? I'll tell you why—because people come here and they're like ''A dollar eighty for soda? I should get it at Food City. But I don't feel like driving there. I'll just buy it here so I don't have to drive up there.'' That's exploiting a weakness, too, isn't it?

DANTE

I can't believe you just rolled a joint in here.

JAY

Hey, man, what happened with that old guy?

DANTE

He died in the bathroom.

JAY

That's fucked up. Yo, I heard he was jerkin' off.

DANTE

I don't know. I wasn't watching.

JAY

Probably saw that Caitlin chick. I know I felt like beatin' it when I saw her.
(pantomimes sex)
Come here, bitch! You like this? Is this what you want? Hunhh?

DANTE

Knock it off. That used to be my girlfriend.

JAY

You used to go out with her?

DANTE

We were going to start again, I think.

JAY

Don't you already have a girlfriend?

DANTE

Veronica.

JAY

Is she that girl who's down here all the time? She came here today carrying a plate of food.

DANTE

Lasagne.

JAY

And what—you were gonna dump her to date that Caitlin chick?

DANTE

Maybe.

JAY

I don't know dude. That Caitlin chick's nice. But I see that Veronica girl doing shit for you all the time. She brings you food, she rubs your back . . . Didn't I see her change your tire one day?

DANTE

I jacked the car up. All she did was loosen the nuts and put the tire on.

JAY

Damn. She sure goes out of her way.

DANTE

She's my girlfriend.

JAY

I've had girlfriends, but all they wanted from me was weed and shit.
(beat)
Shit, my grandma used to say, "Which is better: a good plate with nothing on it . . ." No, wait. I fucked up. She said "What's a good-looking plate with nothing on it?"

DANTE

Meaning?

JAY

I don't know. She was senile and shit. Used to piss herself all the time. C'mon Silent Bob.

Exit JAY. SILENT BOB *stands there.*

SILENT BOB

You know, there's a million fine-looking women in the world, but they don't all bring you lasagne at work. Most of them just cheat on you.

SILENT BOB *leaves.* DANTE *shuts his eyes tightly and rubs the bridge of his nose with his thumb and forefinger, as if in deep concentration. He suddenly snaps his eyes open.*

                    DANTE
               (nearly surprised)
     He's right. I love her.

Cut to:

INT: VIDEO STORE. NIGHT

RANDAL *has a heart-to-heart with* VERONICA.

                    RANDAL
     So that's it. He doesn't love you anymore. He loves Caitlin.

VERONICA *stares, dumbfounded.*

                    VERONICA
     And . . . he told you all of this?

                    RANDAL
     Pretty much. All except the latent homosexuality part—that's just
     my theory.

                    VERONICA
     I . . . I don't know what to say.

                    RANDAL
     Don't hold it against him. He just never got Caitlin out of his
     system. It's not your fault. It's Dante.
               (beat)
     I don't know thing one about chicks. Do you want to cry or
     something? I can leave.

                    VERONICA
     I'm not sad.

                    RANDAL
     You're not?

VERONICA

No, I'm more furious. I'm pissed off. I feel like he's been killing time while he tries to grow the balls to tell me how he really feels, and then he can't even do it! He has his friend do it for him!

RANDAL

He didn't ask me to . . .

VERONICA

After all I've done for that fuck! And he wants to be with that slut? Fine! He can have his slut!

RANDAL

Um, do you think you can give me a lift home tonight?

VERONICA
(oblivious of RANDAL*)*
I'm going to have a word with that asshole.

VERONICA *storms out.*

RANDAL

Wait! Veronica . . . I don't think . . .

RANDAL *stares after her. A customer stands nearby.*

RANDAL
(to customer)
What am I worried about? He'll probably be glad I started the ball rolling. All he ever did was complain about her anyway. I'm just looking out for his best interests. I mean, that's what a friend does, am I right? I did him a favor.

CUSTOMER
(sees box on counter)
Oooh! *Navy Seals!*

Cut to:

INT: CONVENIENCE STORE. NIGHT

DANTE *is on the ground holding his knee.* VERONICA *stands above him.*

DANTE

What the fuck did you do that for?

VERONICA

If you didn't want to go out with me anymore, why didn't you just say it? Instead, you pussyfoot around and see that slut behind my back!

DANTE

What're you talking about?

VERONICA
(kicks him)

You've been talking to her on the phone for weeks!

DANTE

It was only a few times . . .

VERONICA

And then you pull that shit this morning, freaking out because I've gone down on a couple guys!

DANTE

A couple . . . ?

VERONICA
(throws purse at him)

I'm not the one trying to patch things up with my ex, sneaking around behind your back! And if you think that thirty-seven dicks are a lot, then just wait, mister: I'm going to put the hookers in Times Square to shame with all the guys I go down on now!

DANTE

Would you let me explain . . .

VERONICA

Explain what? How you were waiting until the time was right, and then you were going to dump me for her?

DANTE
(getting up)

Veronica . . . I . . . it's not like that anymore . . . I mean, it was never really like that . . .

VERONICA *kicks him in the other leg.* DANTE *goes down, yelling in pain.*

VERONICA

You're damn right it's not like that! Because I won't let it be like that! You want your slut? Fine! The slut is yours!

DANTE

I don't want Caitlin . . .

VERONICA

You don't know what you want, but I'm not going to sit here anymore holding your hand until you figure it out! I've encouraged you to get out of this fucking dump and go back to school, to take charge of your life and find direction. I even transferred so maybe you would be more inclined to go back to college if I was with you. Everyone said it was a stupid move, but I didn't care because I loved you and wanted to see you pull yourself out of this senseless funk you've been in since that whore dumped you, oh so many years ago. And now you want to go back to her so she can fuck you over some more?

DANTE

I don't want to go back with her . . .

VERONICA

Of course not; not now! You're caught, and now you're trying to snake out of doing what you wanted to do. Well, I won't let you. I want you to follow through on this, just so you can find out what a fucking idiot you are. And when she dumps you again—and she will, Dante, I promise you that—when she dumps you again, I want to laugh at you, right in your face, just so you realize that that was what you gave up our relationship for!
(grabs her purse)
I'm just glad Randal had the balls to tell me, since you couldn't.

DANTE
(weakly)

Randal . . . ?

VERONICA

And having him tell me . . . that was just the weakest move ever. You're spineless.

                         DANTE
          Veronica, I love you . . .

                        VERONICA
          Fuck you.

VERONICA exits. DANTE lies on the floor alone. Cut to:

EXT: VIDEO STORE. NIGHT

RANDAL exits and locks the door behind him. Cut to:

INT: CONVENIENCE STORE. NIGHT

Tight on RANDAL'S face as he steps inside.

                         RANDAL
          Dante?

*Hands clasp around his throat and yank him out of the frame. DANTE
throttles RANDAL, choking him to the ground. RANDAL throws his fists
into DANTE'S midriff, throwing him back into the magazine rack.
RANDAL jumps to his feet as DANTE comes at him again. RANDAL
tumbles into the cakes as Entenman's products scatter beneath and
around him. He grabs a pound cake and hits DANTE in the head with it,
using the opportunity to scurry down the middle aisle. DANTE leaps at
his feet, and RANDAL grabs the shelves, knocking aspirin over until
RANDAL—shrieking—sprays something in DANTE'S face. DANTE
paws at his eyes. RANDAL grabs Italian bread and smacks it into
DANTE'S face as he rushes him blindly. DANTE chases him out of the
frame. M&Ms scatter wildly across the empty floor, and the ruckus is
heard OC. Cut to:*

*DANTE and RANDAL later, out of breath, on the floor. RANDAL sits up
against the candy rack, rubbing his neck. DANTE lies on the floor, bacon
held against a sort of swelling eye. Both are pretty banged up. They are
surrounded by a mess of crushed cookies, ripped-open candies, broken
bread, and other damaged goods.*

                         RANDAL
          How's your eye?

DANTE
(reluctantly)
The swelling's not so bad. But the FDS stings.
(beat)
How's your neck?

RANDAL
It's hard to swallow.

They are both silent. Then . . .

RANDAL
You didn't have to choke me.

DANTE
Why the fuck did you tell Veronica that I was going to dump her for Caitlin?

RANDAL
I thought I was doing you a favor.

DANTE
Thanks.

RANDAL

You were saying how you couldn't initiate change yourself, so I figured I'd help you out.

DANTE

Jesus.

Silence. Then . . .

RANDAL

You still didn't have to choke me.

DANTE

Oh please! I'm surprised I didn't kill you.

RANDAL

Why do you say that?

DANTE

Why do I say that? Randal . . . forget it.

RANDAL

No, really. What did I do that was so wrong?

DANTE

What don't you do? Randal, sometimes it seems like the only reason you come to work is to make my life miserable.

RANDAL

How do you figure?

DANTE

What time did you get to work today?

RANDAL

Like ten after.

DANTE

You were over half an hour late. Then all you do is come over here.

RANDAL

To talk to you.

DANTE

Which means the video store is ostensibly closed.

RANDAL

It's not like I'm miles away.

DANTE

Unless you're out renting videos at other video stores.

RANDAL

Hermaphrodites! I rented it so we could watch it together!

DANTE

You get me slapped with a fine, you fight with the customers and I have to patch everything up. You get us chased out of a funeral by violating a corpse. To top it all off, you ruin my relationship. What's your encore? Do you anally rape my mother while pouring sugar in my gas tank?
(sighs)
You know what the real tragedy is? I'm not even supposed to be here today!

RANDAL
(suddenly outraged)

Fuck you. Fuck you, pal. Listen to you trying to pass the buck again. I'm the source of all your misery. Who closed the store to play hockey? Who closed the store to attend a wake? Who tried to win back an ex-girlfriend without even discussing how he felt with his present one? You wanna blame somebody, blame yourself.
(beat, as DANTE)
"I'm not even supposed to be here today."
(whips stuff at DANTE)
You sound like an asshole. Whose choice was it to be here today? Nobody twisted your arm. You're here today of your own volition, my friend. But you'd like to believe that the weight of the world rests on your shoulders—that the store would crumble if Dante wasn't here. Well, I got news for you, jerk: This store would survive without you. Without me either. All you do is overcompensate for having what's basically a monkey's job: You push fucking buttons. Any moron can waltz in here and do our jobs, but you're obsessed with making it seem so much more fucking important, so much more epic than it really is. You work

in a convenience store, Dante. And badly, I might add. And I work in a shitty video store. Badly, as well.
> *(beat)*

You know, that guy Jay's got it right—he has no delusions about what he does. Us? We like to make ourselves seem so much better than the people that come in here, just looking to pick up a paper or—God forbid—cigarettes. We look down on them, as if we're so advanced. Well, if we're so fucking advanced, then what are we doing working here?

RANDAL gets up, leaving DANTE to contemplate his strong words alone. Cut to:

DANTE and RANDAL silently clean up, backs to each other. Cut to:

DANTE places a mop in the corner. RANDAL pulls on his coat.

> **RANDAL**
> I threw out the stuff that got broken. The floor looks clean.

> **DANTE**
> You need a ride?

> **RANDAL**
> *(looks out door)*
> Got one. Just pulled up.

They stand in silence. Then . . .

> **DANTE**
> Do you work tomorrow?

> **RANDAL**
> Same time. What about you?

> **DANTE**
> I'm calling out. Going to hit the hospital—see how Caitlin is. Then try to see Veronica.

> **RANDAL**
> You wanna grab something to eat tomorrow night . . . after I get out of here?

DANTE

I'll call you. Let you know.

RANDAL

All right. Good luck with Veronica. If you want, I can talk to her, you know, and explain . . .

DANTE

No thanks, I'll take care of it. We've got a lot of shit to talk about.

RANDAL

Helluva day.

DANTE

To say the least.

RANDAL

Do you need a hug or something? 'Cause I would have no hang-ups about hugging you . . . you know, you being a guy and all. Just don't knead my ass when you do it.

DANTE

Get the fuck outta here already.

RANDAL

I'm gone. I'll talk to you tomorrow.

RANDAL *exits. A second later, he reenters and tosses* DANTE *the sheet-sign.*

RANDAL

You're closed.

He exits. DANTE *pushes the sign over from Open to Closed.*

DANTE *climbs behind the counter. He pops the register open and starts counting the drawer out. The door is heard opening.*

POV JOHN: DANTE *counting out the register, not looking up.*

DANTE

What'd you forget something?
                    (looks up, surprised)
Oh. I'm sorry, we're closed.

A gunshot blasts out. DANTE *flies back, his chest exploding. He stares ahead and slumps to the floor.*

JOHN *walks behind the counter, stepping over* DANTE'S *body on the floor, and takes the money out of the register. He grabs a paper bag and jams the money in it. He grabs handfuls of change, shoves it in his pocket, and then quickly exits the frame.* DANTE *continues to lie on the floor, unmoving.*

CREDITS.

Credits end, and the door is heard opening. A customer comes to the counter and stands there. He waits, looks around for a clerk, looks down the aisles.

CUSTOMER

Hello? Little help?

No reply. He looks around again, and glances at the door to make sure nobody's coming in. Then he reaches behind the counter and grabs a pack of cigarettes. He leaves.

cast

Dante	**BRIAN O'HALLORAN**
Randal	**JEFF**
Veronica	**MARILYN GHIGLIOTTI**
Caitlin	**LISA SPOONAUER**
Jay	**JASON MEWES**
Silent Bob	**KEVIN SMITH**
Willam the Idiot Manchild	**SCOTT MOSIER**
Chewlies Rep	**SCOTT SCHIAFFO**
Old Man	**AL BERKOWITZ**
Woolen Cap Smoker	**WALT FLANAGAN**
Egg Man	**WALT FLANAGAN**
Offended Customer	**WALT FLANAGAN**
Cat-Admiring Bitter Customer	**WALT FLANAGAN**
Sanford	**ED HAPSTAK**
#812 Wynarski	**LEE BENDICK**
Hunting Cap Smoking Boy	**DAVID KLEIN**
Low-I.Q. Video Customer	
Hubcap Searching Customer	**DAVID KLEIN**
Coroner	**PATTI JEAN CSIK**
Administer of Fine	**KEN CLARK**
Indecisive Video Customer	**DONNA JEANE**
Caged Animal Masturbator	**VIRGINIA SMITH**

Dental School Video Customer	**BETSY BROUSSARD**
Trainer	**ERNEST O'DONNELL**
Alyssa's Sister Heather	**KIMBERLY LOUGHRAN**
Angry Hockey-Playing Customer	**SCOTT MOSIER**
Tabloid-Reading Customer	**GARY STERN**
Cat-Shit-Watching Customer	**JOE BAGNOLE**
Olaf the Russian Meathead	**JOHN HENRY WESTHEAD**
Stuck in Chips Can	**CHUCK BICKEL**
Jay's Lady Friend	**LESLIE HOPE**
''Happy Scrappy'' Mom	**CONNIE O'CONNER**
Hockey Goalie	**VINCENT PERIERA**
Engagement Savvy Customer	**VINCENT PERIERA**
''Happy Scrappy'' Kid	**ASHLEY PERIERA**
Bed-Wetting Dad/	
Cold-Coffee Lover	**ERIX INFANTE**
Video Confusion/	
Candy Confusion Customer	**MELISSA CRAWFORD**
Blue-Collar Man	**THOMAS BURKE**
Door-Tugging Customer	**DAN HAPSTAK**
Leaning Against Wall	**MITCH COHEN**
Burner Looking for Weed	**MATTHEW BANTA**
Cut-Off Customer	**RAJIV THAPER**
Orderly	**KEN CLARK**
Customer with Diapers	**MIKE BELICOSE**
Customer with Vaseline	**JANE KURITZ**
and Rubber Gloves	
MilkMaid	**GRACE SMITH**
Angry Mourners	**SCOTT MOSIER**
	ED HAPSTAK
	DAVE KLEIN
Little Smoking Girl	**FRANCES CRESCI**

Angry Crowd at Door	**MELISSA CRAWFORD**
	MATT CRAWFORD
	SARLA THAPAR
	LESLIE HOPE
	MITCH COHEN
	DAVID KLIEN
Hockey Players	**BRIAN DRINKWATER**
	BOB FISLER
	DEREK JACCODINE
Angry Smoking Crowd	**MATTHEW PERIERA**
	FRANK PERIERA
	CARL ROTH
	PAUL FINN
Dog	**HAIKU**
Cat	**LENIN'S TOMB**
Edit	**SCOTT MOSIER**
	KEVIN SMITH
Initial Incompetent Sound Editor	**SCOTT MOSIER**
Accomplished Sound Editor	**JAMES VON BUELOW**
Master Sound Mixer	**JAMES VON BUELOW**
Sync Fix	**JOIA SPECIALE**
Music	**BENJI GORDON**

''CLERKS''

Written by: S. Smyth and S. Angley

Performed by: Love Among Freaks

''KILL THE SEX PLAYER''

Written by: Girls Against Boys

Performed by: Girls Against Boys

Courtesy of Touch and Go Records

"GOT ME WRONG"
Written by: J. Cantrell
Performed by: Alice In Chains
Courtesy of Columbia Records

"MAKING ME SICK"
Written by: T. Stinson, G. Gershunoff, R. Bradbury
Performed by: Bash and Pop
Courtesy of Sire Records by arrangement with Warner Special Products

"CHEWBACCA"
Written by: Art, Hank, Dave
Performed by Supernova

"GO YOUR OWN WAY"
Written by: Lindsey Buckingham
Performed by: Seaweed
Courtesy of Sub Pop Records

"PANIC IN CICRO"
Written by: The Jesus Lizard
Performed by: The Jesus Lizard
Courtesy of Touch and Go Records

"SHOOTING STAR"
Written by: Paul Rodgers
Performed by: Golden Smog
Courtesy of Crackpot Records

"LEADERS AND FOLLOWERS"
Written by: G. Graffin
Performed by: Bad Religion
Courtesy of Atlantic Recording Corp., and Sony Music, a group of Sony Music
Entertainment, Inc.

"VIOLENT MOOD SWINGS" (Thread Mix)
Written by: W. Fickus, C. Hall, J. Sellers, D. Suycott, S. Zuchman
Performed by: Stabbing Westward
Courtesy of Columbia Records

"BERSERKER"
Written by: S. Smyth, S. Angley and K. Smith
Performed by Love Among Freaks

"BIG PROBLEMS"
Written by: R. Mullen and W. Weatherman
Performed by: Corrosion of Conformity
Courtesy of Sony Music

"CAN'T EVEN TELL" (Theme from *Clerks*)
Written by: D. Pirnet
Performed by: Soul Asylum
Courtesy of Columbia Records

Soundtrack Available on Chaos/Columbia Records

Postproduction Supervisor
CHARLIE McLELLAN

Camera Operator	**DAVID KLEIN**
Lighting Assistant	**ED HAPSTAK**
Occasional Camera Assistant	**VINCENT PERIERA**
Occasional Grips	**VINCENT PERIERA**
	RAJIV THAPAR
Gaffer	**ED HAPSTAK**
Trouble Shooter	**ED HAPSTAK**
Sound Mixer	**SCOTT MOSIER**
Boom	**WHOEVER GRABBED THE POLE**
Makeup	**LESLIE HOPE**
Cat Wrangler	**VINCENT PERIERA**
Occasional Continuity	**TARA DAUST**
Production Stills	**ED HAPSTAK**
Catering	**QUICK STOP CONVENIENCE**
Cameras by	**PRO CAMERA AND LIGHTING**
Sound Mixed at	**SOUND HOUND**

Title by	**REI MEDIA GROUP**
Postproduction Equipment by	**SPERA GROUP**
Legal Eagle	**JOHN SLOSS**
Czar of Representation	**JOHN PIERSON**

thanks

Quick Stop Convenience

R.S.T. Video

Jan Film Lab

Steve and Choice Video

Postens Funeral Parlor

First Avenue Playhouse

Film Video Arts

Bubba Shea

Mr. and Mrs. Hapstak

Traci Lapanne

Leonardo First Aid

Kenneth Schneider

John and Carol Mosier

Butch and Mary Lou King

Tim Hill and the Borough of Highlands

The New School for Social Research

Henry Hudson Regional

The Doonsbury Company

D.C. Comics

Maysle's

Sound One

Magno

The Residents of Leonardo

Amy Taubin

Peter Broderick

David Linde

Larry Kardish

Geoff Gilmore

Janet Pierson

the director would like to thank

God—For the gifts

Mom and Dad—For all the support

Scott—For accepting an invitation to lunch

Walt—For a copy of "Dark Knight Returns"

Ed—For being a Magpie

Kim—For seven years

Kristin—For patience, perseverance and love

Vincent—For the inspiration

Dave—For all the pretty pictures

Jason—For being Jason

Bry—For taking nothing seriously

Virginia—For saying "Be a filmmaker"

Brother Don—For always picking up the check

Toni and Landmark—For all the possibilities

Mr. and Mrs. Thapar—For being as understanding as parents

Ann and Andy—For the cash

Karen Lapointe—For the note

Larry Baroujian—For not turning me in

John "My Hero" Pierson—For having second thoughts

Bob Hawk—For having nothing better to do on 10/3/93

Mark "Doctor Love" Tusk—For not giving up

Harvey Weinstein—For an unforgettable order of potato skins

and

Hal Hartley, Richard Linklater

Spike Lee and Jim Jarmusch—For leading the way.

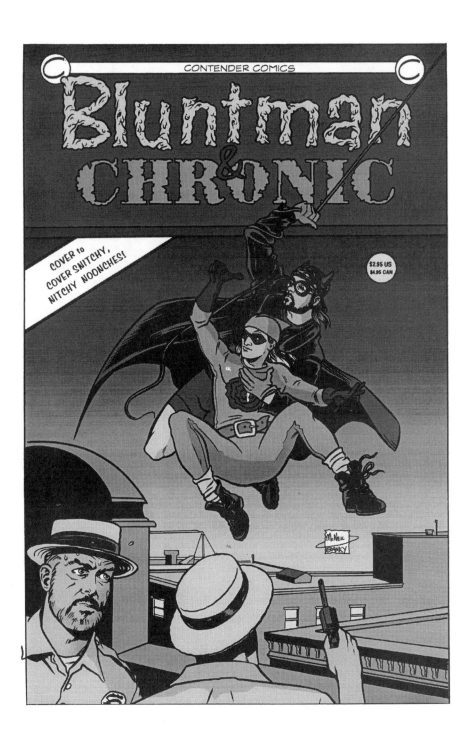

OUR STORY BEGINS AS ALWAYS IN FRONT OF THE LEONARDO STORES...

THIS IS MY DONNIE WAHLBERG MOVE!

SUDDENLY...

HOLY SHIT! LOOK!

THE BLUNT SIGNAL!

THAT ONE-EYED FUCKWAD MUST BE UP TO NO GOOD AGAIN! LET'S GO!

AND QUICKER THAN WALT FLANAGAN'S DOG, THE MILD-MANNERED DOPE-DEALERS BURST THROUGH THE DOOR OF R.S.T. VIDEO...

HEY!

GANGWAY, YOU COCK-SMOKIN' CLERK!

EVIL'S AFOOT!

...PAST THE CHILDREN'S TAPES AND ADULT TITLES, IN SEARCH OF...

...ONE VERY SPECIAL BOX, THAT WILL GIVE THEM ACCESS TO...

IF I KNOW DERRIS, HE'S PROBABLY HEADED TOWARD MILLER BEACH! WE CAN HEAD HIM OFF ON SOUTH PEAK STREET!

AND FROM THE BLUNT-CAVE RUSHES THE SOMNOMBULIC DUO, AS BLUNTMAN STEERS THE AWESOME MIGHT OF THE BLUNTMOBILE INTO YET ANOTHER BOUGHT OF COSTUMED COMBAT...

...WITH HIS MORTAL ENEMY!

THERE HE IS, DUDE!

RICK FUCKING DERRIS!

PLBBHHTTT!!

FUCK YOU BITCHES!

DUDE, IT'S A GOOD THING THIS CAR IS ALL SORTS OF TRICKED-OUT, BECAUSE THIS CALLS FOR THE PANIC BUTTON!

CLICK

THE SWORN DUTY OF THE PAIR IS TO PROTECT THE TRI-TOWN AREA FROM CHAOS WITH WIT, BRUTE FORCE, AND A WONDEROUS ARRAY OF GADGETS.

POP

BUT FIRST THINGS FIRST...

AHHH...THE PAUSE THAT REFRESHES...

NOW LET'S SEE...HOW ABOUT THIS ONE!

AS THE SAYING GOES--IF MUHAMMED CAN'T GO TO THE MOUNTAIN...

THEN THE MOUNTAIN MUST GO TO MUHAMMED.

SHIT, RICK! THEY'VE SWITCHED TO THE BLUNT-WING!

WHERE DO THEY GET THOSE WONDERFUL TOYS?!

PEEK-A-BOO, DINGLEBERRIES.

THE CAPTAIN HAS JUST TURNED ON THE DROP YOUR PANTS SIGN...

BECAUSE YOU'RE ABOUT TO TAKE IT...

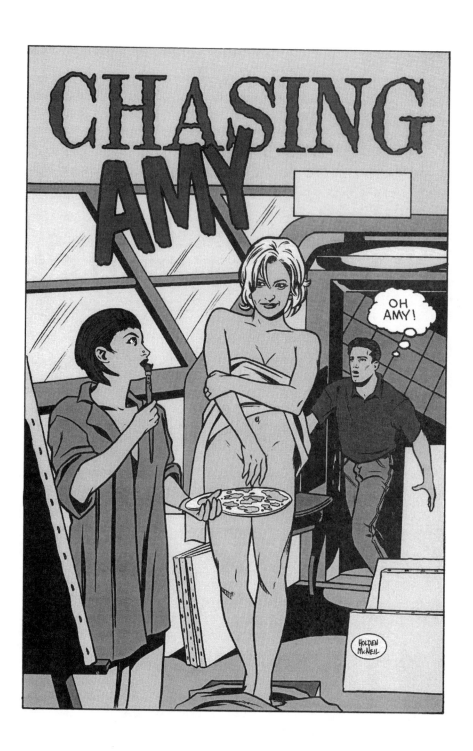

chasing
AMY

INT: COMIC BOOK STORE. DAY

A pile of comic books is on a shelf next to myriad others. The most prominent one is called Bluntman and Chronic. *A hand reaches in and pulls one out of frame.* HOLDEN *opens the comic and flips through it. He shakes his head.* BANKY *looks over his shoulder.*

> BANKY
>
> Felt like this fucking day would never come. Issue two—on the shelf.

> HOLDEN
>
> Yippee.

> BANKY
>
> I mean, how often does a guy get the opportunity to purchase something with his name on it?
> > *(points to name on cover)*
>
> Banky Edwards—right?
> > *(points to the other)*
>
> Holden McNeil.

> HOLDEN
>
> I know my name.

> BANKY
> > *(beat)*
>
> Wah, wah, wah.

> HOLDEN
>
> Wah, wah, what?

BANKY

Wah, wah, you. You and your commercial self-loathing. We've
got nothing to be ashamed of. We've got the rest of our lives to
be artists.

HOLDEN

(off comic)

All I'm saying is this is easy, all right? And right now it pays the
bills. But let's not forget that we're better than this.

BANKY

All right.

(beat)

But I'll tell you who we *are* better than: these two fags over here.

They approach the counter, where STEVE-DAVE, *the store manager, and*
WALT, *the* FAN-BOY, *play a card game.*

BANKY

(lays books on the counter)

All right, Old Maids—take a break from the Crazy Eights
marathon and ring us up.

STEVE-DAVE

(not looking up)

Well, well, well, Walt. Did you see who it is? The local celebrities.
Quick—get them to autograph one of their books so we can sell
it for triple its value.

WALT

I'm not that in need of fifteen cents right now.

They snicker and high-five one another. Holden rolls his eyes.

BANKY

You know, you guys operate the smallest ladies' bridge circle I've
ever seen.

WALT

For your information, we're playing Crimson Mystical Mages—
an overpower card game. Not that either of you would give a shit
about something as advanced as this—there are no dick or poopie
jokes involved.

BANKY

(to Holden)

I don't think they're fans.

WALT

No, we're not. You're both a couple of fucking no-talents that got lucky.

STEVE-DAVE

And obviously your handlers or hangers-on convinced you that your first comic was good, which it was not—it was thoroughly mediocre with a few spiky bits of dialogue. And when you get your foot in the door of the business, what do you do? You turn out a piece of shit like *Bluntman and Chronic*.

WALT

Tell him, Steve-Dave.

STEVE-DAVE

(off comic)

Bluntman and Chronic. Pah. What was that thing the little stoner pulled on the villain in the last issue?

WALT

The Stinky-palm.

STEVE-DAVE

The Stinky-palm. You give comics a bad name. Whenever one of my customers comes in, I tell them *not* to buy it—to spend their money on a *real* comic book.

WALT

Fucking one-hit wonder, dime-store Frank Millers.

STEVE-DAVE

This is the reality at Comic-Toast—you're not going to get your ass kissed here, because both me and Walt think you suck.

WALT

And me.

STEVE-DAVE

I said that.

STEVE-DAVE *offers the boys his two middle fingers, then goes back to playing his game with Walt.* HOLDEN *and* BANKY *stare, shocked.* BANKY *nudges* HOLDEN *and they both exit.* STEVE-DAVE *and the* FAN-BOY *slap hands and go back to playing.*

WALT

I've got a dragon card—forty power-ups and twelve life points! Ha! I get your elf card!

STEVE-DAVE

You're such a bitch! But thankfully, I've saved a dark forces Shaman card for just such an occasion.

WALT

You suck! Eighty-six life-power points to my twenty-two!

STEVE-DAVE

I schooled their asses, now I'm schooling yours.

Suddenly, a trash can crashes through the front window. STEVE-DAVE *and* WALT *hit the deck like bitches, covering one another. They look up slowly.* STEVE-DAVE *leaps to his feet and looks at the shattered mess. He pulls something off the trash can and reads it.*

WALT

HOLY SHIT! You know it was those two fucks! Let's call the cops and have them busted! I know where their studio is! Or better yet, let's sue! You can sue them, Steve-Dave!

STEVE-DAVE
(still reading note)
That won't be necessary.

WALT

What? Why the hell not?

STEVE-DAVE
(holds up check)
Because this is a check for three times what that window cost.
(reading note)

"Dear critics—thanks for the insight. But like my grandmother always said—'Fuck 'em if they can't take a joke . . . and break their window.' Kiss it, Banky the Hack. P.S.—I'm rich."

WALT

He said, "Kiss it"?

CREDITS

INT: COMIC BOOK CONVENTION SIGNING BOOTH. DAY

A physically large FAN—sweaty brow, tote bag bursting with comics—leans forward, smiling.

FAN

Could you sign it "To a really big fan"?

Holden sits at a table, across from the barely-managing-to-stand FAN. He offers him a patronizingly kind half-smile in return.

HOLDEN

You bet.

We're at a Comic Book show, specifically at a book signing. Behind Holden hangs a large banner heralding HOLDEN MᶜNEIL AND BANKY

EDWARDS—CREATORS OF BLUNTMAN AND CHRONIC. *Beside it is a large mock-up of the comic book cover, which features two stoner super-heroes who bear a striking resemblance to a pair of very familiar friendly neighborhood drug dealers. Holden hands the book back to the* FAN.

FAN

I love this book, man! This shit's awesome. I wish I was like these guys—getting stoned, talking all raw about chicks and fighting supervillains! I love these guys! They're like Cheech and Chong meet Bill and Ted!

HOLDEN

I like to think of them as Rosencrantz and Guildenstern meet Vladimir and Estragon.

FAN

Yeah!

(beat)

Who?

BANKY *signs the book of another* COLLECTOR.

COLLECTOR

So, what do you, like, draw this or something?

BANKY

I ink it and I'm also the colorist. The guy next to me draws it. But we both came up with the characters.

(calling out)

Next.

COLLECTOR

What's that mean—you "ink it"?

BANKY

Well, it means that Holden draws the pictures in pencil, and then he gives it to me to go over in ink. Next.

COLLECTOR

So basically, you just trace.

Banky freezes. He composes himself and continues signing.

BANKY

It's not tracing, all right. I add depth and shading to give the image more definition. Only then does the drawing truly take shape.

COLLECTOR

You go over what he draws with a pen—that's tracing.

BANKY
(hands book back to COLLECTOR*)*

Not really.
(calling out)

Next!

A LITTLE KID *steps up, but the* COLLECTOR *lingers.*

COLLECTOR
(to LITTLE KID*)*

Hey man, if somebody draws something and then you draw the exact same thing right on top of it, not going outside the designated original art, what do you call that?

LITTLE KID
(shrugs)

I don't know. Tracing?

COLLECTOR
(to BANKY*)*

See?

BANKY

It's not tracing.

COLLECTOR

Oh, but it is.

BANKY
(to LITTLE KID*)*
Do you want your book signed or what?

COLLECTOR

Hey—don't get all testy with him just because you have a problem with your station in life.

BANKY

Oh, I'm secure with what I do.

COLLECTOR

Then just say it—you're a tracer.

BANKY
(grabbing LITTLE KID'S book)
How should I sign this?

LITTLE KID
(grabs book back)
I don't want you to sign it, I want the guy that *draws* Bluntman
and Chronic to sign it. You're just a tracer.

COLLECTOR

Tell him, Little Shaver.

Holden accepts a comic from another FAN.

HOLDEN
(off comic)
Who do I sign it to?

Before HOLDEN *can finish, a loud crash is heard. He looks to his left
and freaks.* BANKY *is throttling the* COLLECTOR *from across the table.
The* COLLECTOR *attempts to fight him off.* SECURITY GUARDS *pull
them apart.* HOLDEN *grabs* BANKY.

COLLECTOR

YOU'RE MUCKING WITH A "G," YOU FUCKING
TRACER!

BANKY
(to COLLECTOR)
I'LL TRACE A CHALK LINE AROUND YOUR DEAD
FUCKING BODY, YOU FUCK!

HOLDEN
(to SECURITY GUARD)
Could you get him out of here?

The SECURITY GUARDS *drag the* COLLECTOR *away.*

COLLECTOR

Hey, wait a second! He jumped *me*!
(exiting)
You fucking tracer!

BANKY
(calling OC)
YOUR MOTHER'S A TRACER!

HOLDEN

Can I explain the audience principle to you? If you insult and
accost them, then we have no audience.

BANKY

He started it! Fucking cock-knocker! He's lucky I didn't put my
pen through his thorax!

HOLDEN

Need I remind you . . .
(holds up watch)
Curtain's in ten minutes.

INT: COMIC BOOK CONVENTION LECTURE HALL. DAY

HOOPER *fills the frame. He comes off like a typical, pro-Black/anti-White
homeboy.*

HOOPER

For years in this industry whenever an African-American
character—hero or villain—was introduced—usually by *white*
artists and writers—they got slapped with racist names that
singled them out as negroes: Black Panther, Black Lightning,
Black Goliath, Black Manta, Black Talon, Black Spider, Black
Hand, Black Falcon, Black Cat . . .

VOICE FROM CROWD

She's white.

HOOPER

She is?
(beat)
Well, bust this—regardless.

We're at a panel discussion. The room is full. Five creators sit at a long table, their names on placards in front of them. (One of them is a very striking GIRL.) The banner behind them reads WORDS UP—MINORITY VOICES IN COMICS.

HOOPER
(holds up comic)
Now my book, *White-Hating Coon,* doesn't have any of that bullshit. The hero's name is Maleekwa, and he's a descendant of the black tribe that established the first society on the planet, while all you European motherfuckers were still hiding in caves and shit, all terrified of the sun. He's a strong role model that a young black reader can look up to. 'Cause I'm here to tell you—the chickens are comin' home to roost, ya'll: The black man's no longer gonna play the minstrel in the medium of comics and Sci-Fi/Fantasy! We're keeping it real, and we're gonna get respect—by any means necessary!

During the speech, HOLDEN *and* BANKY *enter and sit up front.*

HOLDEN
(calling out)
That's a bunch of bullshit! Lando Calrissian was a black man, and he got to fly the *Millennium Falcon!*

HOOPER *whips his head around, looking for the source of the comment.*

HOOPER
Who said that?

HOLDEN
(standing)
I did! Lando Calrissian is a positive black role model in the realm of Science Fiction/Fantasy.

HOOPER
Fuck Lando Calrissian! Uncle Tom nigger! Always some white boy gotta invoke "the holy trilogy"! Bust this—those movies are about how the white man keeps the brother man down—even in a galaxy far, far away. Check this shit: You got Cracker farmboy Luke Skywalker; Nazi poster boy—blond hair, blue eyes. And then you've got Darth Vader: the blackest brother in the galaxy. Nubian God.

BANKY

What's a Nubian?

HOOPER

Shut the fuck up! Now Vader, he's a spiritual brother, with the Force and all that shit. Then this cracker Skywalker gets his hands on a light-saber, and the boy decides he's gonna run the fucking universe—gets a whole *Klan* of whites together, and they're gonna bust up Vader's 'hood—the Death Star. Now what the fuck do you call that?

BANKY

Intergalactic Civil War?

HOOPER

Gentrification. They're gonna drive out the black element, to make the galaxy quote, unquote safe for white folks.

HOLDEN

But Vader turns out to be Luke's father. And in *Jedi*, they become friends.

HOOPER

Don't make me bust a cap in your ass, yo! *Jedi*'s the most insulting installment, because Vader's beautiful, black visage is sullied when he pulls off his mask to reveal a feeble, crusty old white man! They're trying to tell us that deep inside, we all want to be white!

BANKY

Well, isn't that true?

HOOPER *explodes. He pulls a nine millimeter from his belt, draws on* BANKY *and fires.* BANKY *goes down, falling forward into the crowd. The crowd screams and starts to scatter.* HOOPER *jumps over the table and raises his fists in the air.*

HOOPER

BLACK RAGE! BLACK RAGE! I'LL KILL ANY WHITE FOLKS I LAY MY MOTHERFUCKIN' EYES ON!

The crowd is gone. HOLDEN *sits in his chair, laughing.* HOOPER *steps off the stage and picks* BANKY'S *head up off the floor.*

HOOPER
(breaking character)
''What's a Nubian?'' Bitch, you almost made me laugh!

HOOPER *sounds different. Actually, he sounds gay. Actually—he is.*
BANKY *smiles.*

BANKY

Well, what about you? You didn't tell me you were going to scream "Black Rage." I nearly pissed myself.

HOLDEN

How do you manage to get away with this all the time? Shouldn't cops be busting your head open right about now?

BANKY

Wrong coast.

HOOPER
(off gun)

Well this right here—she full of blanks, okay. And Opiate gets all sorts of legal clearances before I go on.

HOLDEN

Your publisher actually condones these theatrics?

HOOPER

Condones? Honey, they insist. I need to sell the image to sell the book. Would the audience still buy the "Black Rage" angle if they found out the book was written by a . . . a . . .

BANKY

Faggot.

HOOPER

When you say it, it sounds so sexy . . .
(he kisses BANKY full on the lips)

BANKY
(wipes his lips)
Hey, hey! I'll play your victim, but not your catcher.

VOICE

How is it that you sound like Minister Farakhan when you're on stage . . .

They turn to see . . .

a beautiful, blonde, ruffled-haired angel swinging her purse in a circle. Her name is ALYSSA. She's the striking GIRL from the panel who didn't get to say much.

ALYSSA

. . . and the King of Pop when you're not.

HOOPER

Look out, boys—this kitten has a whip.

ALYSSA

(shoves and slaps him)

Always before I get to speak! I swear—the next con I attend and they ask me to be on the minority panel, if I see your name anywhere near the list, I'm passing.

HOOPER

(defending himself)

Holden, Banky—this pile of PMS is Alyssa Jones. She does that book *Idiosyncratic Routine*. This is the fourth panel we've been on together, and even though she knows my publisher sets this up and pays for the event, she still gets mad when it ends with my act.

ALYSSA

I just wish I was the one who gets to shoot you.

HOOPER

That's what my father said when I came—nay—leapt out of the closet.

(*off guys*)
These boys do *Bluntman and Chronic,* which outsells both of our books put together, hence they're never on a panel with the likes of us. They slumming right now.

BANKY

I've read your book. It's cute. Chick stuff, but cute.

Holden hits him.

BANKY

What?

HOLDEN
(*shoots him a look; to Alyssa*)
Sorry about him. He's dealing with being an inker.

ALYSSA
(*to Banky*)

Oh. You trace?

Banky seethes.

HOLDEN
(*shaking her hand*)
I really enjoy your book. I'm surprised we've never met at any other cons before.

ALYSSA

Lose the dick or change your skin tone and we can get to know each other on panel after panel . . . Meanwhile the Pink Black Panther here can play Chuck D. for the fan-boys.

HOOPER

Hey, jealousy.
(to the BOYS)
I promised Alyssa I'd buy her a post-rave drink. Do the Garden-Staters have to sprint to the Lincoln Tunnel, or can you stay for a round in the big, scary city?

BANKY

We're gonna take off soon . . .

HOLDEN

We'll go.

BANKY *offers* HOLDEN *a puzzled glance. Then he nods to* HOOPER.

BANKY

We'll go.

He shoots HOLDEN *an angry glare.*

INT: BAR. NIGHT

HOLDEN, BANKY, ALYSSA, *and* HOOPER *sit around a table drinking, talking, and smoking.*

BANKY

Archie, all right? Archie and the Riverdale gang were a pure and fun-lovin' bunch. You can't find dysfunction in those comics, because they were just flat out wholesome.

HOOPER

Archie and Jughead were lovers.
(sips his drink)

BANKY

Shut the fuck up.

HOOPER

It's true. Archie was the bitch and Jughead was the butch—that's why Jughead wears that crown-looking hat all the time: he the king of queen Archie's world.

BANKY

Man, I feel a hate crime coming on.

HOLDEN

He's got a point. Archie never did settle on Betty or Veronica.

BANKY

Because he wanted them both at the same time, you assholes! He never chose *one* because he was trying to get *both* of them into a three-way!

HOOPER
(pulls out a dollar and hands it to BANKY)
Here. I want you to go down to the corner store and buy yourself a clue. Go on.

BANKY

Eat it, Urkel.

HOOPER

I told you to watch it with that Urkel shit. Face it, girl—Archie's a sister.

BANKY
(getting up; to HOOPER*)*
That's it. You.

HOOPER
Moi?

BANKY
Yeah, you. You are marching back across the street with me, and we're going to pick up a shitload of Archie books. I am going to prove to you—beyond the shadow of a doubt—that Archie was all about pussy. Come on.

HOOPER
(sliding out of booth)
This boy is conflicted. I shall play mother-therapist for him. You two sit tight. We shall return promptly.

BANKY *and* HOOPER *exit, leaving* ALYSSA *and* HOLDEN *alone at the table.*

ALYSSA
Is he always like that?

HOLDEN
Who, him? For years now. Started back in third grade—a nun was teaching us about the Blessed Trinity. She's going on about the three persons in one God thing—Father, Son, Holy Spirit. Banky just goes ballistic. They got into this huge fight.

ALYSSA
An eight-year-old kid? Please. How bad could it have been?

HOLDEN
You ever seen a nun call a small child a "fucking cunt-rag"? Wasn't pretty. Shit like that's bound to happen when you make a kid wear a matching tie and slacks every day.

ALYSSA
And *your* parochial school misadventures?

HOLDEN
Limited to wine-tasting prior to Mass. Turned me into a grade-school alcoholic altar boy. I couldn't tell you how many mornings after serious benders I'd wake up next to strange priests.

ALYSSA

Aren't you the sharp wit?

HOLDEN

Sharp? No. I'm just a fan of clergy-molestation humor. Probably why the extended family quit inviting me to First Communion parties.

ALYSSA
(looking OC)

You play darts?

HOLDEN

Not professionally. You know—only in bars.

AT THE DART BOARD

A dart hits the board. Then, one hits the wall beside the board.

ALYSSA *winds up with another dart.* HOLDEN *watches. Hers always hit. His never do.*

ALYSSA

So your new book seems to be selling like mad.

HOLDEN

All goes back to something my grandmother told me when I was a kid. ''Holden,'' she said, ''the big bucks are in dick and fart jokes.'' She was a churchgoer.

ALYSSA

Oh, the cry from the heart of a real artist trapped in commercial hell, pitying his good fortune. I'm sure you can dry your eyes on all those fat checks you rake in.

HOLDEN

I'm sorry—did I detect a note of bitter envy in there?

ALYSSA

Nope. I'm happy my stuff gets read at all. There's very little market for hearts and flowers in this Spandex-clad, big pecs, big tits, big guns field. If I sell two issues, I feel like John Grisham.

HOLDEN
(looking out window)
It's all about marketing. Over- or underweight guys who don't get laid—they're our bread and butter. People like those two outside should be yours.

Through the window, we see a COUPLE *making out on the hood of a car.*

HOLDEN
And sadly, there are more of our core audience.
(smiles)
Look at that, though—kind of gives you a little charge, to see two people in love. And all over Banky's car, no less. You know, that car's seeing more action right now than it's seen in years.

ALYSSA
Bubbly guy like that, it's hard to figure out why.

HOLDEN
(still looking at OC COUPLE*)*
You've gotta respect that kind of display of affection. It's crazy, rude, self-absorbed, but it's love.

ALYSSA
That's not love.

HOLDEN
Says you.

ALYSSA
That out there? That's fleeting.

HOLDEN
Fleeting.

ALYSSA
Uh-huh. You wanna hear about love? Oh, I'll tell you about love.

HOLDEN
A story?

ALYSSA
The story. The *original* love story.

HOLDEN

Doctor Zhivago.

ALYSSA

Nope. My mother's uncle. He was a millionaire.

HOLDEN

Get out.

ALYSSA

I kid you not.

HOLDEN

Explain.

ALYSSA

All through high school, he dated this one girl. They were inseparable. And when they graduated, she went off to Carnegie Mellon . . .

HOLDEN

In Pittsburgh.

ALYSSA

I'm impressed. So he stays in the hometown, and they begin their long-distance relationship. The plan is, on the third Sunday of every month, he'll train out, spend a week, then train back. They do this for four years.

HOLDEN

That is love.

ALYSSA

Not nearly finished. Two months before she's going to graduate, he's got this job digging graves, and he comes across . . .

HOLDEN

A stiff.

ALYSSA

A steamer trunk containing silver ingots.

HOLDEN

Get out of here.

ALYSSA

Many, many silver ingots. Now, my mother's uncle—being quite the ingenious chap—he buries the trunk again and heads up to the main office, where he proceeds to purchase a cemetery plot. Guess which one?

HOLDEN

Clever.

ALYSSA

So now he owns the plot and all of its contents. Two days later, my mother's uncle is worth three million.

HOLDEN

At which time he marries the high school sweetheart and lives happily ever after.

ALYSSA

Not even close. Inside the steamer trunk, stenciled into the wood, or something like that, is a curse.

HOLDEN

Someone wrote *Fuck* inside his new steamer trunk.

ALYSSA

Not that kind of curse. A cryptic curse: "Great fortune means great loss" it said.

HOLDEN

What kind of asshole writes that inside a steamer trunk?

ALYSSA

The same kind of asshole that buries silver ingots. The day my mother's uncle is heading out to see the girl, he stops at his accountant's to grab some cash, and winds up missing his train. So he has to take the next one—which he does—and he gets there an hour later than his usual time of arrival, whereupon he sees lights.

HOLDEN

A hero's welcome for the new millionaire.

ALYSSA

It seems that while she was standing on the platform waiting that extra hour for my mother's uncle to show up, the girl was dragged into the bushes by an unknown assailant, raped, and gutted.

HOLDEN *is silent.* ALYSSA *downs her drink.*

ALYSSA

The assailant was never apprehended.

HOLDEN
(beat)

That's a love story?

ALYSSA

Yes, and here's why: My mother's uncle rode that train every day for the rest of his life. One day up, the next day back. Did that till the day he died. He donated the fortune he'd acquired to the train station in Pittsburgh to have a well-lit terminal built. The train line let him ride for free after that.

HOLDEN

I should hope so. Jesus, that's the saddest tale I've ever heard.

ALYSSA

That's my love story.

ALYSSA *tosses her last dart.* HOLDEN *seems a bit dazed. He looks out the window.*

HOLDEN

Those two aren't on the hood of Banky's car anymore.

ALYSSA

I told you. It wasn't love.
(grabs her purse)
Well, I gotta split. It was really nice meeting you. Good luck with your book.
(shakes his hand)
Tell Hooper I'll call him later. And tell your friend to calm down.

ALYSSA *exits to the right.* HOLDEN *stares after her.*

(OC) HOOPER

Shut up, already.

(OC) BANKY

Man, you shut up!

Two beats later, HOOPER *and* BANKY *enter, holding an* Everything's Archie *comic between them.*

BANKY

You're insane. Archie is *not* fucking Mister Weatherbee!

HOOPER

Deny, deny, deny.
                    (to HOLDEN*)*
Where's Alyssa?

HOLDEN

Huh? Oh. She left. She said she'd call you later.

BANKY
(off comic)
He's just offering to help Archie with his homework!

HOOPER

Read between the lines.

BANKY
(shoves book at him)
Fuck this.
                    (to HOLDEN*)*
Let's go. Traffic.
                    (no response from HOLDEN*)*
Holden!

HOLDEN
(shaken)
What?

BANKY

Let's go.

HOOPER
(looking out window)
D'jou see that dent in the hood of your car?

BANKY
(looking out window)
Son of a bitch!

BANKY *runs out.* HOLDEN *shrugs at* HOOPER.

HOOPER
Let me guess: You like her?

HOLDEN
Who?

HOOPER
Miss Alyssa Jones.

HOLDEN
She's all right.

HOOPER
As long as that's all.
(lights smoke)
Maybe you can convince that partner of yours to drop me off
downtown before you scurry out the tunnel?

HOLDEN
(beat)
Mr. Weatherbee wasn't really trying to fuck Archie, was he?

They begin exiting.

HOOPER
Hell, no. Weatherbee was Reggie's bitch.

INT: STUDIO. DAY

We're in HOLDEN *and* BANKY'S *studio/apartment. It's a rented loft
place with high ceilings, wood floors, and sparse furnishings. There are
posters on the walls, a sort of kitchenette, a big TV (with all the
trimmings—VCR, laser-disc player, Sega, SNES), a huge comfy couch,*

and two drawing boards with adjacent desks (littered with pencils, pens, coloring pencils, paints, erasers, etc.)—at which sit HOLDEN *and* BANKY. *They're working. Some music plays.*

CU of HOLDEN *penciling—over his shoulder, we see* HOLDEN *sketching Chronic in midattack of his archnemesis—the* GIGGLER. HOLDEN *erases a line and redraws.*

CU of Banky *inking—over his shoulder, we see* BANKY *outlining a prepenciled page. He traces* BLUNTMAN *swinging from a streetlight.*

The two work in silence. Then . . .

> BANKY
> *(not looking up)*
> This is one of the best streetlights you've ever drawn.

> HOLDEN
> It's the one across the street from the post office.

> BANKY
> Looks just like it.

> HOLDEN
> Thanks.
> *(beat)*
> What do you wanna do tonight?

> BANKY
> I don't know. Get a pizza. Watch *Degrassi Junior High.*

> HOLDEN
> *(erases)*
> You got a weird thing for Canadian melodrama.

> BANKY
> I've got a weird thing for girls who say ''aboot.''

The phone starts ringing. HOLDEN *answers it, while still drawing.*

> HOLDEN
> Bank hold up.

Crosscut between HOLDEN *and* HOOPER. *He's on a phone in a club.*

HOOPER

Hooper here. Listen, I know how you burb-fiends hate the city,
but there's a club shindig going down that I think you'd really get
into.

HOLDEN

Where is it?

HOOPER

Place called Meow Mix. I'm temping as barkeep.

HOLDEN

I don't know, Hoop. We're prepping the next issue, and we've got
that stupid meeting in the morning.

HOOPER

I told her you wouldn't be interested.

HOLDEN

Told who?

HOOPER

Alyssa.

HOLDEN

Alyssa from last night Alyssa?

HOOPER

How do you begin and end a question with the same word like
that? You got skill. Yes, that one. She asked me to invite you.
Now here's the part where you say . . .

HOLDEN

I'll be there.

HOOPER

Thought so. Ten o'clock. Later.
                    (both hang up)

BANKY

Who was that?

HOLDEN

Hooper. He invited me to a club.

BANKY

When's that faggot going to learn—you like chicks.

HOLDEN

(getting up)

Not that kind of a club.

BANKY

So when we leaving?

HOLDEN

"We?" You can't go. He's setting me up with Alyssa.

BANKY

And?

HOLDEN

And I don't want you messing it up.

BANKY

Like I care about your shit. Maybe I'll hook up myself.

HOLDEN

(pulling on coat)

I just told you—it's not that kind of club.

BANKY

How does one man get to be so funny?

HOLDEN

(throws him his coat)

How are you going to get home if I hook up?

BANKY

Like that'll happen.

HOLDEN

Let me explain something to you, my witless chum—the other night, we two—Alyssa and I—we shared a moment.

BANKY

Oh, you had a moment?

204

HOLDEN
(brings his two pointer fingers together)
We *shared* a moment. And in that moment, one thing was made
abundantly clear: This girl loves me, my friend. Loves—me.

INT: HER-STERECTOMY. NIGHT

*It's a club—people are mingling, a band is playing, it's loud. But
something's fishy.*

HOOPER'S *tending bar.* BANKY *enters.*

BANKY
All right—bring on the free hooch.

HOOPER
What do you mean, ''free''? I didn't even invite your tired ass.
(looks around)
So where's your better half?

BANKY
Taking a piss. Guy's got a bladder like an infant.

HOOPER
That's funny—he says you're *hung* like an infant.

BANKY
Must his mother tell him everything?

HOLDEN *enters.*

BANKY
What'd you do—fall in love?

HOLDEN
Where is she?

HOOPER
Over there . . .

On the dance floor—in the middle of a throng of people—dances
ALYSSA. *She moves like a cat and she's looking very sexy.*

(OC) HOOPER
Look at her. Been dancin' for an hour. Hasn't stopped yet.

HOOPER, HOLDEN, *and* BANKY *stare OC.*

BANKY
She ain't no Denny Terrio, I'll say that.

HOLDEN *smacks* BANKY *and moves to exit.*

HOLDEN
If I'm not back by Tuesday, call my mother.

HOOPER
Wait, wait, wait—there's something you should know.

HOLDEN
She's got a boyfriend.

HOOPER
Well . . . no.

HOLDEN
Then what's to know, my friend?
(gazes OC)
What's to know?

HOLDEN *exits. They watch him go.* BANKY *looks around.*

BANKY
There're a lot of chicks in this place.

HOOPER
"Chicks." You're such a man.

BANKY
(beat)
He didn't really say that about my dick, did he?

*On the dance floor—*HOLDEN *slips into the crowd and dances up to* ALYSSA. *He busts a move, intentionally bumping into her.*

HOLDEN
(fake rage)
Hey lady—you fucked up my cabbage patch!

ALYSSA
Well, well, well—if it isn't Bluntman himself. Or should I call
you Chronic?

HOLDEN
Call me flattered. I heard you sent me the invite to this little
soiree.

ALYSSA
From a former hometown girl, to Mister Hometown himself.

HOLDEN
You're saying you're from the 'burbs?

ALYSSA
Middletown, New Jersey.

HOLDEN
Get out of here! I'm from Highlands!

ALYSSA
I know. Hooper told me.

HOLDEN
How is it that we never ran into each other?

ALYSSA
You graduate from Hudson?

HOLDEN
Yeah. Eighty-eight.

ALYSSA
I went to North.

HOLDEN
What a small fucking world! So you know the tri-town area?

ALYSSA
Quiz me.

HOLDEN

Miller Hill?

ALYSSA

I wrote my name on the wall.

HOLDEN

Sandy Hook?

ALYSSA

Lost my virginity there.

HOLDEN

This is so cool. The mall?

ALYSSA

Eden Prairie of Menlo Park?

HOLDEN

Wait—here's the big test: Quick Stop?

ALYSSA

My best friend fucked a dead guy in the bathroom.

HOLDEN

You know that girl?

ALYSSA

I did. Before she was committed.

HOLDEN

You know what this is? This is fate.

ALYSSA
(regarding her move)
No, this is the ''Rog.''

HOLDEN

I was talking about us meeting—what are the chances?

ALYSSA

Pretty slim. I haven't been back to the 'burbs since my friend's
funeral.

HOLDEN
The Quick Stop girl died?

ALYSSA
Another girl—Julie Dwyer. She died in the . . .

HOLDEN
YMCA pool! Damn! You knew her too?

ALYSSA
So well.

HOLDEN
One friend in an asylum, the other friend in the grave. You're a
dangerous person to know.

ALYSSA
But I can tap.
			(does an impromptu tap dance)
That was the Buffalo Two-Step.

HOLDEN
Very solid.

ALYSSA
That's what six years of tap lessons yields.

HOLDEN
Two towns away from each other for years and we had to meet in
New York.

The band stops playing. People clap.

ALYSSA
Could have been worse—we could have not met at all.

HOLDEN *looks at her.*

(OC) SINGER
Okay, we're back. Thank you. Thanks.

The SINGER onstage speaks into the microphone.

SINGER

A long time ago, we used to have this bass player who took off one day to draw funny books or something. Maybe you've seen her stuff—it's called *Idiosyncratic Routine*?

The crowd applauds. ALYSSA, *embarrassed, shakes her head, smiling.* HOLDEN *pokes her.*

SINGER

But what a lot of people don't know is that she used to harbor these delusions that she could sing. And she used to subject us to these throaty renditions of Debbie Gibson tunes and shit, insisting that we let her front on a few numbers. Well, we didn't and she quit . . . and then she got famous, the bitch.
(*crowd laughs*)
So she's here tonight, and I think if we all begged, or maybe offered her some X, she'd get up here and treat us to some of her vocal stylings.
(*crowd applauds*)
What do you say, Alyssa?

ALYSSA *shakes her head no. The crowd urges her.* HOLDEN *pushes her forward.*

SINGER

She's shy.
(*yelling*)
GET UP HERE AND SING, BITCH!!

The crowd thunders. ALYSSA *offers the* SINGER *an embarrassed half-smile. She looks at* HOLDEN, *who claps along with the others and nods toward the stage.* ALYSSA *shakes her head and relents, heading through the crowd.*

BANKY *and* HOOPER *stand at the bar.* HOOPER *cheers.*

BANKY

What am I doing here? This is so fucking gay.
(*he exits*)

HOOPER
(*beat*)
You don't know the half of it.

ALYSSA *jumps onstage, hugging the* SINGER. *She takes the mike, shaking her head. The crowd is applauding.*

ALYSSA

She is such a cunt.

The crowd cheers. ALYSSA *laughs. She turns to the band and says something, to which they nod. She turns back to the crowd.*

ALYSSA

All right. I should dedicate this, right?
(thinks)
This is for that special someone out there.

HOLDEN *smiles.* BANKY *joins him.* HOLDEN *glances at him.* BANKY *offers a mocking mimic of his smile.*

The band starts playing. Cross-cutting begins.

ALYSSA *launches into a torchy tune. The song is extremely sexy—as is* ALYSSA, *who works the mike, making direct eye contact with . . .*

HOLDEN. *Or does she?* HOLDEN *is smiling, being seduced.* BANKY *rolls his eyes. Beside* HOLDEN *stands a pretty* GIRL *with a short haircut, who's also riveted by* ALYSSA'S *performance.* ALYSSA *makes big-time eye contact with somebody out there. The song seems to be aimed at whoever she's looking at. It's more than obvious there's a seduction going on, but of whom? At the end of the song, the crowd goes wild, but* ALYSSA'S *preoccupied. She points to someone in the crowd, and curls*

her finger back in a "c'mere" fashion, urging whoever it is to join her.
She jumps off the stage.

HOLDEN *shakes his head sheepishly and looks downward, aw-shucks*
style. At that moment, the GIRL *beside him leaps forward.* BANKY'S
eyes widen. HOLDEN *looks up and is suddenly taken aback.*

ALYSSA *and the* GIRL *race into each other's arms and fall into a way-*
too-passionate-to-mean-anything-else kiss. HOLDEN'S *eyes bug.*
BANKY *allows a smile to creep across his face. He begins clapping, but*
then looks around, and for the first time, we get the distinct impression
that this is a lesbian bar. There are *a lot of chicks in this place. Gay chicks.*
BANKY *looks at* HOLDEN *and slaps him on the back.*

> BANKY
> Now that, my friend, is a . . .
>> *(brings his fingers together, mimicing* HOLDEN*)*
> . . . shared moment.

HOLDEN *continues to stare—mouth agape.* ALYSSA *and the* GIRL
continue to kiss.

INT: HER-STERECTOMY. LATER

BANKY, HOLDEN, ALYSSA, *and the* GIRL *from the dance floor sit*
around a table. ALYSSA *and the* GIRL *continue to make out.* HOLDEN
and BANKY *casually watch, wide-eyed.* BANKY *stares a little harder.*
HOLDEN *hits him.*

> BANKY
> What?

> HOLDEN
>> *(under his breath)*
> That's rude.

> BANKY
> Man, when are we ever going to get a chance to see this kind of
> shit live without paying for it?

ALYSSA *and the* GIRL *break their kiss.*

> ALYSSA
> Uh-oh—better knock it off: We're getting a man excited.

HOLDEN

Sorry. It's just . . . new to him.

BANKY

Oh, and you're an old hand at this.

ALYSSA

No, I should apologize. I don't usually get all mushy in public.
But it's been a while since I've seen Kim here.

KIM

(formerly the GIRL*)*

Tell me you didn't set that gross display up with the band just so
you could nail me.

ALYSSA

Like I'd have to go through that much effort.

KIM

You know what? I want to dance.

ALYSSA

Go ahead. I'll watch from here.

KIM

(tugging at her arm)

No, I want to dance with *you.*

Don't be such a rag. I have to sit here and work up the desire to
fuck you later.

KIM

Please.

KIM *exits.* BANKY *is smiling ear-to-ear.* ALYSSA *looks at him.*

ALYSSA

Yes?

BANKY

You said "fuck."
          (to HOLDEN*)*
She said "fuck."
          (to ALYSSA*)*
You said "fuck" to that girl. You said you'd "fuck" her.

ALYSSA

And?

BANKY

How can a girl "fuck" another girl? Were you talking about
strap-ons or something?

HOLDEN

Would you shut up?

BANKY

What? It's a valid question. You know the dyke stuff in the
Penthouse Letters section is written by guys—this is our chance
to get the inside scoop.

HOLDEN
          (to ALYSSA*)*
I don't know how many times I can apologize for him.

ALYSSA

It's okay.
          (to BANKY*)*
No, Banky—I've never used a strap-on.

BANKY

Then what's with saying ''fuck''? Shouldn't you say ''eat her out'' or at least modify the term ''fuck'' with something like ''fist''?

ALYSSA

Let me ask you a question—can men ''fuck'' each other?

BANKY

Are you asking for my permission?

ALYSSA

In your estimation.

BANKY

Sure.

ALYSSA

So for you, to ''fuck'' means to penetrate. You're used to the more traditional definition—you inside some girl you've duped, jackhammering away, not noticing that bored look in her eyes.

BANKY

Hey—I always notice the bored look in their eyes, all right.

ALYSSA
(laughs)

''Fucking'' is not limited to penetration, Banky. For me it describes any sex when it's not totally about love. I don't love Kim, but I'll fuck her. I'm sure you don't love every girl you sleep with.

BANKY

Some of them I downright loathe.

ALYSSA

But I'll bet it's different with the ones you love. I'll bet you go the full nine when it's not just a quick fix—like you'll go down on them longer.

HOLDEN

Here we go.

BANKY

I don't do that.

ALYSSA

What?

BANKY

I stopped dropping. It got to be too frustrating.

HOLDEN

As stupid as you usually come off during this little diatribe of
yours, you're going to come off ten times as stupid on this
occasion.

BANKY

What? I lost my tolerance for the bullshit baggage that comes
with eating girls out. What's the big deal?!

ALYSSA

If you say the smell, so help me, I'll slug you.

BANKY

Not the smell—the smell is good. I'm talking about not being
able to do it properly. And my mother brought me up to believe
that if I can't do something right, I shouldn't do it at all. Of
course, my father told me she gave lousy head, but that's beside
the point.

ALYSSA

At least you blame yourself for your sexual inadequacies.

BANKY

No, I blame them. Chicks never help you out. They never tell you
what to do. And most of them are all self-conscious about that
smell factor, and so most of the time they just lie there, frozen
like a deer in the headlights, right? Not for nothing, but when a
chick goes down on me, I let her know where to go, and what the
status is. You gotta handle it like CNN and the Weather
Channel—constant updates.

HOLDEN

You're such an idiot.

ALYSSA

No, he's got a point. That's how I was in high school—all nervous, and inhibited about being eaten out. But by the time I got to college, that all changed. I loosened up. Not only did I learn to communicate—I learned to be bossy. I was like one of those guys at the airport with those big flashlights—waving them this way, directing them that way, telling them when to stop.

BANKY

And that's all I'm saying. It'd be different if chicks helped out—pointed a guy in the right direction. Then there'd be no bullshit, no wasted time, and no chance for permanent injuries.

ALYSSA

Permanent injuries?

BANKY

Sure. You wanna see something permanent?
(pulls out front tooth)
See that? I got that from Nina Rollins.

At this point, the stories they tell are illustrated in black-and-white flashbacks.

BANKY

Sophomore year—I'm going down on her, right. And out of nowhere, her cat jumps on her stomach, and she does this big ol' pelvic thrust—cracks my tooth in half, sends it down my throat. I had to get a crown for the stub.

ALYSSA
(to HOLDEN)
I got that beat.
(to BANKY)
I got that beat.
(half-turns and lifts shirt)
Junior year. I'm going down on Cynthia Slater in her dorm room after we went club hopping. I'm totally drunk, and in the middle of it, I fall asleep—right there in her lap. She got so mad, she digs her heel into my back, right there.
(points to scar)
That's permanent.

BANKY

All right. See this?
(moves neck slightly right)
That's the farthest I can move my neck to the right. Again,
sophomore year. I'm going out with Brandi Svenning. And for
like six months, I'm going down on her, and not a damn thing's
happening. Then one night, I change a position, or vary my
lapping speed, and suddenly it's a whole new world. She's
moving around, convulsing, breathing heavy. And her legs are
pressing against my ears so tightly that I don't hear her father
come into the room. He grabs my hair . . .
(grabs his own hair and pulls back)
and he pulls me way back, hard.

ALYSSA

(throws up her leg and rolls up pants)
Senior year. Spring Formal. I'm eating out Missy Kurt in her
brother's car. She's lying across the backseat, and I'm half-
hanging out of the car, my knees on the ground. She's flailing
around, and she knocks the parking brake off. The car starts
rolling down the hill, and my left knee is cut up to shit—like a
kiddy's scissor class cut it up for paper dolls.

BANKY *and* ALYSSA *laugh.* HOLDEN *looks at a small scar on his arm
and thinks better about mentioning it. Then* KIM *reenters and plants a big
kiss on* ALYSSA'S *neck.*

HOLDEN

(off a watch that isn't there)
Holy shit, look at that time. We've gotta beat traffic.

BANKY

What traffic—it's one-thirty in the morning!

HOLDEN

(getting up)
And rush hour starts in six hours. Let's go.
(to ALYSSA*)*
Thanks for inviting us out. It was . . . educational.

ALYSSA *waves at him as he exits.* BANKY *slides out of the booth.*

BANKY
(to KIM*)*
Since you like chicks, right . . . do you just look at yourself naked
in the mirror all the time?

HOLDEN *reaches in and pulls* BANKY *out.* ALYSSA *watches them go,
then turns and kisses* KIM.

INT: ALTERNA-MUSIC CHANNEL'S OFFICE WAITING ROOM. DAY

HOLDEN *looks preoccupied.* BANKY *flips through magazines, biting off
mini pieces of the gum he's chewing. He sticks them between pages,
presses the magazine closed, picks up another one and then repeats the
whole process. A* RECEPTIONIST *types.* HOLDEN *stares at* BANKY.
BANKY *meets his stare.*

BANKY
What?

HOLDEN
(off BANKY'S *endeavor)*
Grow up.

BANKY
(patronizingly)
Ohhh, why are you in such a bad mood? You're still dwelling on
that dyke?

HOLDEN
Knock it off.

BANKY
What'd I tell you—she just needs the right guy. All every woman
really wants—be it mother, senator, nun—is some serious deep-
dicking.

The RECEPTIONIST *stops typing and looks at* BANKY, *shocked.*

BANKY
(off her look)
Sorry.

The RECEPTIONIST *goes back to typing.* BANKY *shrugs at* HOLDEN.

BANKY

See, that's why I can't buy lesbians. Everyone needs dick. See, I can buy fags. Bunch of guys that need dick, you know—just plain need it? That I get. But dykes? Bullshit posturing. But, live and let live, I guess.

HOLDEN

I'm sure the gay community appreciates your support.

JOHN SLOSS, *the boys' lawyer, joins them.*

SLOSS

Tell me you haven't blown this deal already.

BANKY

Sloss like a motherfucker.
(*slaps his hand*)

SLOSS

Every mother but *yours*—a shyster's gotta have his standards. Shall we?

INT: ALTERNA-MUSIC CHANNEL EXEC'S OFFICE. DAY

The EXECS *are a casual couple of guys, sitting across from our trio.*

EXEC 1

We just want to start off by saying that it's a real pleasure to finally meet you. While it's been—shall we say—an experience dealing with Sloss here, one of the main reasons we started this whole thing was to meet the guys that do *Bluntman and Chronic.*

EXEC 2

(*points at them*)
''Snootchie-bootchies.''

The EXECS *and* SLOSS *laugh.* HOLDEN *and* BANKY *politely join in.* BANKY *shoots* HOLDEN *a "these guys are idiots" look.*

EXEC 1

Which brings us to our proposal: We are extremely interested in doing twelve, half-hour *Bluntman and Chronic* cartoons. The

days of Butthead are over, we're looking for something . . .
something . . .

BANKY
Even more retarded and juvenile to sate the voracious,
intellectually challenged miscreants that make up your key
demographic.

The EXECS *laugh hard.* SLOSS *secretly shrugs to* BANKY *and gives the
thumbs up.*

EXEC 1
(composes himself)
So what do you say? Are we in business?

BANKY *leans back into the couch, wearing a thoughtful face. He looks
to* HOLDEN, *then to* SLOSS. SLOSS *nods in understanding.*

SLOSS
Jim, Sean—could we have a few minutes?

EXEC 2
(looks to EXEC 1*)*
Uh . . . absolutely. We'll just . . .

EXEC 1
Uh . . . wait outside.

The EXECS *smile and head out, closing the door behind them.* SLOSS
turns to BANKY.

SLOSS
So? Did I do good?

BANKY
You did better—you sold us out!

They clasp hands and quietly explode in ebullience.

SLOSS
Do you know how much you'll make on merchandising alone?

BANKY
(as Simon Bar Sinister)
Money and power, and money and power . . .

SLOSS
(joins in)
. . . and money and power, and money and . . .

HOLDEN
(interrupting)
I don't think it's a good idea.

BANKY *and* SLOSS *freeze. They stare at* HOLDEN.

BANKY
What's not a good idea? Please don't say the cartoon, please don't
say the cartoon . . .

HOLDEN
The cartoon.

SLOSS
What? Are you out of your fucking mind?

BANKY
(getting up)
John, let me handle this.
(to HOLDEN*)*
You *are* out of your fucking mind, aren't you?

HOLDEN
Is this how you want to be remembered? As the guy who created
Bluntman and Chronic?

BANKY *sits at the* EXEC'S *desk and starts rifling through the guy's stuff.*

BANKY
No, I'd like to be remembered as the filthy *rich* guy who created
Bluntman and Chronic.

HOLDEN
It'll be all glossy and mainstream. We'll lose any artistic
credibility we ever had.

SLOSS
(to BANKY*)*
Is it me? I don't see the problem.

BANKY
(to Sloss)
He just has to get over this crush of his.

SLOSS
Oh God—not on Carrie Fisher again?
(to HOLDEN*)*
Holden, she's not really a princess.

BANKY
(opening drawer with a letter opener)
Not on her; on Alyssa Jones—the chick that does that comic book
Idiosyncratic Routine. You ever seen it?

SLOSS
Please. Like I even read *your* comic, let alone anyone else's.
(to HOLDEN*)*
I'm not limited to offering you legal counsel only, my friend. I'm
also learned in the ways of the heart and can offer you this
advice—nail her, get it out of your system, and move on. Like we
say at Sloss Law—good fences make good neighbors.

BANKY
She'd never let him in her yard. The chick's gay.

SLOSS
(laughing)
She's gay? You fell for a *gay,* comic-book-writing chick? Holden,
you poor, poor man!
(beat)
Wait a sec—does she have representation?

BANKY
Always working, you.
(holds up a Polaroid of a naked woman)
Look at this—that guy Jim's wife has a string of pearls hanging
out of her ass.

SLOSS

Would you leave his stuff alone!

(to HOLDEN)

You can break her resolve, killer. All it takes is one good man. But if it takes two good men, don't hesitate to call me. That being said, in regards to the more pressing issue, I suggest you leave the art to the museums and grab on with both hands to the big, fat check.

HOLDEN

I'll give it some thought.

BANKY

(holding up Polaroid)

I'm taking this as a precaution—just in case they give us any shit about pussy's decision delay.

(glaring at HOLDEN)

You'll "give it some thought." You're so retarded.

HOLDEN

I'm retarded? This from the guy who only forty-five minutes ago paid fifty bucks for what's supposed to be a bootleg of *March of the Wooden Soldiers* with a deleted scene of Stan Laurel wearing a French Tickler.

SLOSS

How'd you fall for that?

BANKY

The guy who sold it to me had an honest face.

INT: STUDIO. DAY

There is a door. There's a knock at the door. HOLDEN *opens it and* ALYSSA *is standing there.*

ALYSSA

Hi. Somebody told me that they make comic books here—which is so weird because I have this great idea for a story. It's about a guy who comes to this club and hightails it when he finds out—ready for this—this girl is gay. Any interest in a story like that?

HOLDEN *smiles.*

EXT: RIVERFRONT PARK. DAY

ALYSSA *and* HOLDEN *walk through the park, eating hot dogs.*

> ALYSSA
>
> An animated series?

> HOLDEN
>
> Twelve episodes.

> ALYSSA
>
> That's great, isn't it?

> HOLDEN
>
> Banky seems to think so.

> ALYSSA
>
> But you don't.

They come to a swing set and sit down on the swings.

> HOLDEN
>
> I don't know if that's the perception I want people to have of our stuff. I know this sounds pretentious as hell, but I like to think of us as artists. And I'd like to get back to doing something more personal—like our first book.

> ALYSSA
>
> Well, when are you going to do that?

> HOLDEN
> *(beat)*
>
> As soon as we have something personal to say.

> ALYSSA
>
> Do you know how pretty you are?

> HOLDEN
>
> What?

> ALYSSA
>
> You're a pretty man.

HOLDEN
Uh . . . thanks.

ALYSSA
Oh, I get it. I'm into girls, so I have to find all men repulsive or something.

HOLDEN
I didn't say anything.

ALYSSA
Aren't there some men that you find attractive? Granted, not enough to sleep with, but still—just handsome or something?

HOLDEN
Sure. Harrison Ford. And our mailman.

ALYSSA
Well, it's the same thing. I look at you and just find you really handsome. And you know, it has very little to do with your look, per se. Your look is fine, don't get me wrong. But it's more your outlook. The things you say, the way you see things. It's . . . I don't know . . . attractive.

HOLDEN *looks away, embarrassed.*

ALYSSA
I weirded you out the other night.

HOLDEN
Huh? No, not really.

ALYSSA
Come on.

HOLDEN
(beat)
It's just that I've never seen that kind of thing up close and personal. It just took a while to process, longer than usual.

ALYSSA
Do you want to talk about it?

HOLDEN

If you want to.

ALYSSA

I like you. I haven't liked a man in a long time. And I'm not a man hater or something. It's just been some time since I've been exposed to a man that didn't immediately live into a stereotype of some sort. And I want you to feel comfortable with me, because I want us to be friends. So if there are things you'd like to know, it's okay to ask me.

HOLDEN
(beat)

Okay. Why girls?

ALYSSA
(beat)

Why men?

HOLDEN

Because that's the standard.

ALYSSA

If that's the only reason you're attracted to women—because it's the standard . . .

HOLDEN

It's more than that.

ALYSSA

So you've never been curious about men?

HOLDEN

Curious about men? Well . . . I always wondered why my father watched *Hee-Haw*.

ALYSSA

You know what I mean.

HOLDEN

No.

ALYSSA

Why not?

HOLDEN

No interest.

ALYSSA

Because . . . ?

HOLDEN

Girls feel right.

ALYSSA

And that's how I feel. I've never really been attracted to men. I'm more comfortable with the idea of girls.

HOLDEN

Wait, wait, wait—you're still a virgin?

ALYSSA

No.

HOLDEN

But you've only been with girls.

ALYSSA

You're saying a person's a virgin until they've had intercourse with a member of the opposite sex?

HOLDEN

Isn't that the standard definition?

ALYSSA

Again with your standards. I think virginity is lost when you make love for the first time.

HOLDEN

With a member of the opposite sex.

ALYSSA

Why? Why only then?

HOLDEN

Because that's the standard.

ALYSSA

So if a virgin is raped, then she's still a virgin?

HOLDEN

Of course not.

ALYSSA

But rape is not the standard. So she's had sex, but not the standard idea of sex. Hence, according to your definition, she'd still be a virgin.

HOLDEN

Okay, I'll revise. Virginity is lost when the hymen is broken.

ALYSSA

Then I lost my virginity at ten, because I fell on a fence post when I was ten, and it broke my hymen. Now I have to tell people that I lost it to a wooden post I'd known my whole young life?

HOLDEN

Okay, second revision—virginity is lost through penetration.

ALYSSA

Physical penetration or emotional?

HOLDEN

Emotional penetration?

ALYSSA

Well, I fell in love hard with Caitlin Bree when we were in high school.

HOLDEN

Physical penetration.

ALYSSA

We had sex.

HOLDEN

Yeah, but not real sex.

ALYSSA

I move to have that remark stricken from the record, on account of it makes you come off as completely naïve and infantile.

HOLDEN

Well, where's the penetration in lesbian sex?

ALYSSA *holds up her hand.*

HOLDEN

A finger? Come on. I've had my finger in my ass, but I wouldn't say I've had anal sex.

ALYSSA

Observe.

ALYSSA *mimes fisting.* HOLDEN *is aghast.*

HOLDEN

You're kidding!

(*she nods*)

How . . . ?

ALYSSA

Our bodies are built to pass a child, for Christ's sake.

HOLDEN

But doesn't it hurt?

ALYSSA

Sure. But in a good way. And it's only a once-in-a-while thing—reserved for really special occasions.

HOLDEN

What about not-so-special occasions?

ALYSSA

Tongue only.

HOLDEN

But how can that be enough? I mean, let's be real—how big can a tongue even get?

ALYSSA *swallows what she's chewing and releases her tongue, which is just huge.* HOLDEN *is transfixed. Alyssa wraps it back up and smiles, standing.*

ALYSSA

Let's go.

She exits. HOLDEN *remains on the swing.* ALYSSA *comes back in.*

ALYSSA

Come on.

HOLDEN

Just . . . uh . . . just give me a minute.

INT: TRAIN STATION—DAY

HOLDEN *enters.* BANKY *tries to balance way too much luggage.*

HOLDEN

Look at you. It's a two-day trip.

BANKY

I got the Sega in one bag, my clothes in the other, and two months' worth of unread comics in this one.

HOLDEN

We're going to a convention, for the love of God. We'll be busy from ten till eight each day. When are you possibly going to have time for any of that shit? In fact, fuck it—you're leaving some of this shit here in a locker. Come on—give me the two that aren't clothes.

BANKY

Hold on.
                    (starts rifling through one bag)

HOLDEN

What are you doing?

BANKY

I just have to get something.
                    (pulls out a huge stack of porno books)

HOLDEN

Who are you, Larry fucking Flynt? What are you going to do with all of those?

BANKY

Read the articles. What do you think I'm going to do with them?
They're stroke books.

HOLDEN

You've got like thirty books in there! We're only going to be gone
for two days!

BANKY
(leafing through mags)
Variety's the spice of life. I like a wide selection. Sometimes I'm
in the mood for nasty close-ups, sometimes I like them arty and
air-brushed. Sometimes it's a spread brown-eye kind of night,
sometimes it's girl-on-girl time. Sometimes a steamy letter will
do it, sometimes—not often, but sometimes—I like the idea of a
chick with a horse.

A beeping sound is heard. HOLDEN *checks his beeper.*

HOLDEN

Go check us in. I've gotta call Alyssa.

BANKY

His master's voice.

HOLDEN

Put that stuff away.

HOLDEN *exits.* BANKY *starts packing his magazines up. A little* KID
enters, staring at him.

BANKY
(notices KID; beat)
Hi.

HOLDEN *finishes dialing the phone. Cross cut between him and* ALYSSA
at home.

ALYSSA

I hope for the sake of the women you've dated that you're only
this quick in returning calls.

HOLDEN

What's up? I'm about to get on a train.

ALYSSA

Ohhh. Why?

HOLDEN

Last-minute invite to the Boston Con.

ALYSSA

Shit.

HOLDEN

What?

ALYSSA

My sister's at my parents'. I was gonna go see her.

HOLDEN

The one that wrote the book?

ALYSSA

Yeah. But I was staying all weekend, and I wanted to hang out
with you. This sucks.

HOLDEN
(thinks)
You know—*both* of us don't have to go.

ALYSSA

Really?

HOLDEN

Yeah. Banky can go by himself. It's not like we're on a panel. It
was just a signing appearance.

ALYSSA

If you come pick me up, I'll be your best friend.

HOLDEN
(beat)
Where's your apartment?

ALYSSA

I'm not there. I'm at a friend's—in the Village. Corner of Houston
and Mercer. Number eighty-six, apartment 6-D.

HOLDEN

I'll be there in half an hour.

ALYSSA

You're so easy.

They hang up. HOLDEN *reacts to something OC and exits quickly.*
BANKY *points to pictures in the book. The kid looks on.*

BANKY

. . . And then Black Beauty couldn't take it any longer, and *he*
finally did some of his *own* mounting.

HOLDEN *grabs* BANKY'S *arm and drags him away.*

HOLDEN

What are you doing?

BANKY
(waving to KID*)*
I think I want kids of my own one day. They're fun.

HOLDEN

Listen to me—I'm not going. You're going to have to do this one
by yourself.

BANKY

What? Why?

HOLDEN

Alyssa's coming down for the weekend, so I want to hang out
with her. You don't need me for this.
(taking his excess baggage)
Meantime, I'll take this stuff home. You can keep the filth. I'll
pick you up at nine Sunday night, all right? Don't forget to plug
the *Annual* and don't mention the TV show, okay? Call me if you
get bored.

And he's gone. BANKY *stands there, openmouthed.*

EXT: APARTMENT 6-D. DAY

HOLDEN *knocks at the door. It opens. A* WOMAN *is standing in the
doorway in her bra. She looks* HOLDEN *up and down and smirks.*

HOLDEN

Hi. I'm here to pick up Alyssa.

WOMAN

Let me guess—"the right man"?

HOLDEN

Excuse me?

WOMAN

You've got it in your head that Alyssa's not really into
chicks—that she just hasn't met the right man. And you believe
you're it. That is so cute. You're going to treat her right, fuck her
like a stud, and "straight-jacket" her back from the land of the
lost. And the sad truth is that you'll accomplish none of that and
wind up as either an even more bitter misogynist or a reverse fag-
hag.

HOLDEN *is at a loss.* ALYSSA *slips past the* WOMAN, *carrying an
overnight bag.*

ALYSSA

Don't mind her. That's just her way of saying hello.

WOMAN

Actually, it's just my way of saying, "Give it up."

ALYSSA
(to WOMAN)

You're such an asshole.

WOMAN

When you file the date-rape charges, don't say I didn't warn you.

HOLDEN
(holding out hand)

Hi. I'm Holden, by the way.

WOMAN

I'm the voice of reason that Miss Bitch is having such a hard time
listening to.

HOLDEN

Look, we're just friends.

WOMAN

That's what every guy says before he tries putting your hand on his dick.

HOLDEN

And how do you know men so well?

WOMAN

Because I lap-dance for a living, dickhead.

She slams the door. HOLDEN *looks to Alyssa.*

ALYSSA

Ohhh—you look so cute!

She heads down the stairs.

HOLDEN

Who was that?

ALYSSA

Just an occasional friend.

HOLDEN

Why would you want to hang out with someone as bitter as that?

ALYSSA
(stops)

Remember this?
(sticks out huge tongue)
Hers is even bigger than that.

She smiles and continues on. Holden looks back up at the door. He sticks his own tongue out and sizes it with his fingers.

EXT: TURNPIKE. DAY

The car sits in traffic.

INT: CAR. DAY

HOLDEN *sighs.* ALYSSA *plays with the radio.*

ALYSSA

You were raised Catholic, right?

HOLDEN

Yeah. You?

ALYSSA

Baptist.

HOLDEN

Really? Did you have a strict upbringing?

ALYSSA

Please. There was no time to be bad—we were too busy saying ''Jesus.''

HOLDEN

You think your upbringing had something to do with your lifestyle choice?

ALYSSA

Somewhere along the line. It's a gradual transition to make—from doing what the majority does to taking a leap of faith and doing what feels more natural. Everything helps—from the way you were handled as a kid, to the way the boys acted in third grade, to the shoes you wore at your freshman prom.

HOLDEN

Shoes?

ALYSSA

Well they were *really* tight.

HANGING OUT MONTAGE BEGINS

1. *In the studio,* HOLDEN *displays some of his artwork to* ALYSSA, *during which she pulls out a cigarette and goes to light it. It's a child-proof lighter, so she's having trouble.* HOLDEN *grows a little frustrated. Finally, he grabs the lighter and pulls the childproof tab out with his teeth.* ALYSSA *stares at him a bit taken aback.* HOLDEN *spits the tab out, and lights* ALYSSA'S *smoke. He then continues with his display.*

2. *At the video store—*HOLDEN *picks a Disney cartoon off the shelf.* ALYSSA *pops out of the Adult Room, holding up two all-chick pornos.* HOLDEN *takes the tape out of* ALYSSA'S *hands.*

3. *In the city,* ALYSSA *tries to drag* HOLDEN *into a subway entrance.* HOLDEN *struggles against the idea.*

4. *In Washington Square Park,* HOLDEN *reads off the* Voice *movie listings.* ALYSSA *looks bored. She spots something OC and exits, unbeknownst to* HOLDEN. *A little* GIRL *who could be a young* ALYSSA *replaces her, staring at* HOLDEN. HOLDEN *looks up, and is then taken aback.*

5. ALYSSA'S *birthday—at her apartment, she sits on the couch, eyes closed.* HOLDEN *enters with a cake.* ALYSSA *opens her eyes and reacts: The cake is a topless rendition of her. She laughs.*

6. HOLDEN *and* ALYSSA *walk through a parking lot, talking. She takes his hand and pulls his arm around her shoulders.* HOLDEN *smiles to himself.*

INT: STUDIO. DAY

HOLDEN *and* BANKY *play EA Sports Hockey on Sega. There's a knock at the door.*

HOLDEN

Come in.

ALYSSA *enters and stands beside them, smiling at their game.*

ALYSSA

I read somewhere that guys who play hockey are merely making up for penile deficiencies by carrying big sticks.

BANKY

I thought you lived in the city? This is like the umpteenth time I've seen you here. Isn't that grounds enough for the little pink mafia to throw you out of their club?

HOLDEN
(hits BANKY; to ALYSSA)

I'll be ready in a second. I just have to school this mouthy second-stringer.

BANKY

Bitch, you're schooling no one.

They play. Cut back and forth between the game and BANKY, HOLDEN, *and* ALYSSA.

HOLDEN
(off game)

What? Do something!

BANKY
(off game)

You fucking cockteaser. I'll knock your fucking teeth out and pass all over your ass.

HOLDEN

Look at how slow you are. Christ, you move like a geriatric.

BANKY
(screaming at screen)

Fuck! You fucking cocksucker, man! These faggots won't do what I tell them to!

HOLDEN

Oh, it's the controller, right? It's always the controller.

BANKY

No, it's these . . . fucking queers on blades that can't accept a fucking pass to save their lives! What period is this?

HOLDEN

Final sixty of the third.

BANKY

Fuck! Look at your fucking guys, they . . . FUCK!!!
(whips controller)
FUCKING COCKSUCKER, MAN! I SWEAR TO GOD!

BANKY *storms away.* ALYSSA *looks at* HOLDEN.

HOLDEN

Imagine if I'd only beaten him by one instead of thirty?

INT: SKEE-BALL ARCADE. DAY

HOLDEN *feeds a couple dollars into the change machine.* ALYSSA *looks on.*

ALYSSA

Explain this again.

HOLDEN

How could you have grown up down the shore and never played skee-ball? What did you do with your youth?

They head toward the skee-ball runs.

ALYSSA

Stayed out late, smoked pot, screwed around.

HOLDEN

Not your grade school years; your high school years.

ALYSSA
(off skee-ball run)

This looks complicated.

HOLDEN
(inserts coin and pulls lever)

Jeez, Potzer, the premise is very basic: you roll the ball up the ramp at varying speeds, in an effort to pop it into the score circles. The higher the score, the more prize tickets you get.

ALYSSA

What do you do with the prize tickets?

HOLDEN

You trade them in for prizes that aren't worth nearly as much as you paid to play the game.

ALYSSA

Then what's the point?

HOLDEN

It's fun.

ALYSSA

And you question my lifestyle.

HOLDEN

Observe.

HOLDEN *rolls the ball. It pops into a twenty-point circle.*

HOLDEN

See? It's just that simple.

ALYSSA

Why not just walk up there and put it in the fifty every time?

HOLDEN

Where's the skill in that?

ALYSSA

Oh, this is a skill? I'm sorry, I had no idea.

HOLDEN

Just toss one.

ALYSSA *picks up a ball, squints to aim, and whips it overhand. It pops off one of the circles and shoots back at them, missing them as they duck. An OC knock and an "OW!" is heard. HOLDEN reacts as ALYSSA laughs.*

HOLDEN
(to OC guy)
I'm sorry, man. She's new at this . . .

HOLDEN *ducks as the ball comes sailing back at his head. He gets up.*

HOLDEN
(to OC)
Thank you.
        (hands ALYSSA another ball)
Underhand. Throw it underhand.

ALYSSA

And this is where you take straight chicks on dates.

HOLDEN

It's like Spanish fly. This'll probably be the first time I don't score afterward.

ALYSSA

I don't know. I'm starting to get a tingle in my bottom.
(tosses a ball)
Ten.

HOLDEN

(grabs a ball)
So what'd you do last night?
(prepares to throw)

ALYSSA

Got laid.

HOLDEN whips the ball in surprise. It ricochets off the ceiling and through the glass of an old pinball machine. ALYSSA laughs. HOLDEN looks around, nervously.

ALYSSA

Some more of that skill you were telling me about.

HOLDEN

Maybe we should just leave before somebody gets hurt.

ALYSSA

No way. I want a cheap prize.
(throws a ball)
So your friend's quite the homophobe.

HOLDEN

He just feels left out, I think.

ALYSSA

I'm not talking about his infantile hang-up with me. I'm talking about when you two were playing that game. Every time he swore—when his players messed up, he called them cocksuckers, he referred to the players as queers, he called you a cockteaser . . .

HOLDEN

I thought he was talking to you.

ALYSSA

I know you think it means nothing, and it may in fact be
unintentional, but it's ugly all the same.

HOLDEN

He was just pissed he was losing.

ALYSSA

So he slams the gay community?

HOLDEN

C'mon. Don't get all PC on me.

ALYSSA

I'm not. But what is that saying?

HOLDEN

It says he gets too easily frustrated.

ALYSSA

It's passive/aggressive gay-bashing.

HOLDEN

How do you figure?

ALYSSA

How casually did it roll off his tongue? And that's how he
expresses his anger? By calling people faggots?

HOLDEN

I think you're reading too much into it.

ALYSSA

I think you're just so used to it that it rolls off your back. I've
heard the two of you play your little rankout game where one
insists the other is gay.
                    (as the boys)
"You're a faggot. No, *you're* a faggot." It's cute and all to watch
you go at it like grade schoolers, but it's also offensive—labeling

and ducking the label of being gay as if it were the scarlet fucking letter.

                    HOLDEN
You're blowing this way out of proportion. We live in a more tolerant age now. You refer to yourself as a dyke. Hooper calls himself a faggot all the time . . .

                    ALYSSA
Yeah, but that's what's known as empowerment/disempowerment. I call myself a dyke so it's not too devastating when some throwback screams it at me as I'm leaving a bar at night. Same for Hooper—by calling himself a faggot, he steals the thunder away from the mouthy jerks of this world who'd like to beat him to it. But the difference between us saying it and your friend saying it is miles wide. We say it to mask the pain—you say it for lack of a better expression at any given moment. No Holden, we do *not* live in a more tolerant age. And if you think that's the case, then you've been in the suburbs way too long.

HOLDEN *kind of sulks.* ALYSSA *notices.*

                    ALYSSA
But you know what?
                    (picks up his face)
I have more faith in you than that.
                    (rips her tickets off)
Come on—I want my cheap prize.

INT: STUDIO. NIGHT

HOLDEN *enters.* BANKY'S *still playing Sega.* HOLDEN *sits next to him.*

                    HOLDEN
                    (off screen)
How bad do you suck?

                    BANKY
How was your pseudo-date?

                    HOLDEN
Leave it alone.

BANKY

That chick bugs me.

HOLDEN

(rubs his head; in baby talk)

Aww. Everyone bugs you.

BANKY

Get off.

(off game)

Fucking faggot! Did you see that?! Your dyke-courting ass just got me scored on!

HOLDEN

(beat)

You know, you should watch that. If you're going to get all bent out of shape while playing the game, so much so that you need to curse the TV, try not to gay-bash it, all right? You're not that kind of guy.

(gets up)

And don't call her a dyke, all right? She's a lesbian.

HOLDEN *goes to his drawing table and takes off his coat.* BANKY *sits there, shocked. He puts the controller down and crosses to the drawing table.*

BANKY

What the fuck is going on here?

HOLDEN

(pulling out pencil)

I'm starting a new page.

BANKY

(smacking pencil away)

Not with this shit! With you. What the fuck is going on with you and that girl?

HOLDEN

We're just friends.

BANKY

She's programming you.

HOLDEN

I beg your pardon? Programming?

BANKY

Yeah. And apparently you don't even realize it. What does it matter if I refer to her as a dyke, or if I call the Whalers a bunch of faggots in the privacy of my own office, far from the sensitive ears of the rest of the world?

HOLDEN

It's passive/aggressive gay-bashing; and I know you're not really prejudiced at heart. You should just find some other way to express your anger, is all I'm saying.

HOLDEN *starts drawing. Banky stares at him. Then he grabs the pencil out of* HOLDEN'S *hand and shoves him to the side. He starts drawing something.*

HOLDEN

What are you doing?

BANKY

Bear with me here. I just want to put you through this little exercise.
                    (drawing feverishly)
Okay, now see this? This is a four-way road, okay?

BANKY *draws a four-way Stop. He illustrates according to his voiceover.*

BANKY (VO)

And dead in the center, is a crisp, new hundred-dollar bill. Now at the end of each of the streets, are four people, okay? You following? Up here, we got a male-affectionate, easy-to-get-along-with, nonpolitical agenda lesbian. Okay? Now down here, we have a man-hating, angry-as-fuck, agenda-of-rage, bitter dyke. To this side, we got Santa Claus, right? And over to this side—the Easter Bunny.

BANKY *finishes drawing.* HOLDEN'S *shaking his head.*

BANKY

Which one's going to get to the hundred-dollar bill first?

HOLDEN

What is this supposed to prove?

BANKY

I'm serious. This is a serious exercise. It's like an SAT question.
Which one's going to get to the hundred-dollar bill first—the
male-friendly lesbian, the man-hating dyke, Santa Claus, or the
Easter Bunny?

HOLDEN

(beat; then pissed)

The man-hating dyke.

BANKY

Good. Why?

HOLDEN

I don't know.

BANKY

BECAUSE THESE OTHER THREE ARE FIGMENTS OF
YOUR FUCKING IMAGINATION!

HOLDEN *storms away.* BANKY *follows.*

HOLDEN

I don't need this.

BANKY

She's fucking with your mind, man! She knows you've got this
schoolboy crush, and she's using it to sway your way of thinking!

HOLDEN

And why would she need to do that? What is she—Mata fucking
Hari?! What does she gain?

BANKY

Maybe she thinks you'll get her comic picked up by Contender.
Or maybe she thinks you'll change the content of our book to
something more political and message oriented. Or, gee—I don't
know—maybe because that's just what dykes like to do: fuck
around with straight guys' heads! And then she can run back to
her little rug-muncher club and have a good laugh with all her

man-hating, harpy cronies about how fucking stupid and easily duped men are!

                         HOLDEN
You're so out of line right now . . .

                         BANKY
You don't even know this girl! Big deal, she's from Middletown and she went to North! All the girls at North were bitches and sluts anyway! And this one's got them beat by a mile because she's a bitch/slut/dyke!

                         HOLDEN
Watch your fucking mouth, is all I'm going to tell you . . .

                         BANKY
Oh why? Do you get my back when she bashes me? Because I know she does. And do you know why she does? Because I won't play her fucking game!

                         HOLDEN
Sometimes your paranoia and suspicious bullshit is amusing. Sometimes it's just fucking annoying as piss!

                         BANKY
What is it about this girl? You know you have no shot at getting her into bed! Why do you bother wasting time with her? Because you're Holden fucking McNeil—most persistent traveler on the road that's *not* the path of least resistance! Everything's gotta be a fucking challenge for you, and this little relationship with that bitch is a prime example of your fucking condition. Well, I don't need a fucking magic eight ball to look into your future; you want a forecast? Here—will Holden ever fuck Alyssa?
          (shakes and looks at imaginary ball)
What a shock—''Not fucking likely''! This relationship of yours is affecting you, our work, and our friendship, and the time's going to come when I throw down the gauntlet and say it's me or her! And then what're you going to say?!

                         HOLDEN
                         (beat)
I think you should let this one go.

BANKY

No, what would you say? Would you trash twenty years of
friendship because you've got some idiotic notion that this chick
would even let you sniff her panties, let alone fuck her?

HOLDEN

Let it go, asshole . . .

BANKY

What the fuck, man? WHAT THE FUCK MAKES THIS BITCH
ALL THAT IMPORTANT?

HOLDEN *looks at* BANKY *for a long beat.*

HOLDEN

I'M FUCKING IN LOVE WITH HER, MAN! OKAY?

BANKY *stares at him.* HOLDEN *stares back.* BANKY *softens a bit and
drops his head.*

BANKY

Fuck.

BANKY *walks away.* HOLDEN *watches him go.*

INT: DINER. NIGHT

HOLDEN *and* ALYSSA *sit at a booth.* ALYSSA *picks through her food.*
HOLDEN *looks at the check and pulls money from his wallet.*

HOLDEN

I wish you were the one being pursued for the cartoon.

ALYSSA

Oh really?

HOLDEN

Sure. Then you could sell out and maybe pick up the check once
in awhile.

ALYSSA
(drops her fork and wipes her hands)
We're leaving?

HOLDEN
Well it's not like this is a bed and breakfast.

ALYSSA
I've got a little business to conduct.

She grabs her bag and slides out of the booth. HOLDEN *watches her, then follows.*

ALYSSA *slides up to the cashier's desk, as does* HOLDEN, *who offers a puzzled shrug.* ALYSSA *offers the "just wait" finger. The* CASHIER *turns to her.*

ALYSSA
Are you an authorized deal maker in this establishment? Do you have the power to negotiate?

CASHIER
You wanna haggle over the price of your French Dip?

ALYSSA
I want to haggle over the price of fine art.

CASHIER
What do you mean?

ALYSSA
(pointing OC)
There. By the kitchen. That painting.

CASHIER
What about it?

ALYSSA
The price tag says seventy-five.

CASHIER
So?

HOLDEN
(to ALYSSA)
Tell me you're kidding?

                              ALYSSA
I'll give you fifty.

                              CASHIER
                              (to OC)
Manuel! Could you bring the Dyksiezski down off the wall?
                          (to ALYSSA)
All my years in the diner business, I've waited for this day—the
day when someone wanted to buy one of the pictures.

                              ALYSSA
                          (holds out hand)
Alyssa Jones. Pleased to meet you.

                              CASHIER
You say you want to haggle, but you don't know rule one about
haggling, which you just broke: You never give your name. The
name is power, and to give the opponent that piece of you is to
give away victory.

                              ALYSSA
I'm only trying to conduct a transaction. We're not opponents.

                              CASHIER
                 (accepting painting from BUSBOY*)*
Oh, but we are—if you think I'm letting this beautiful piece go
for fifty.

                              ALYSSA
Ah-ha!
                          (to HOLDEN)
Now we're haggling.

INT: CAR. NIGHT

It's drizzling outside. HOLDEN *drives.* ALYSSA *hugs her painting and
pushes her bare feet against the windshield, making footprints.*

                              HOLDEN
I've always wondered what kind of people buy those things. I
can't believe you talked him down to twenty-five!

                                251

ALYSSA

It was looking shaky when he told me the artist was a blind
cripple with a humpback, but I held my ground. There's no room
for sympathy in the buyer's market.

HOLDEN

Where are you going to hang it?

ALYSSA

I'm not. You are.

HOLDEN

You want me to hang it for you? You better hope it doesn't get
out to the girl-nation that you needed a man to help you hang a
picture.

ALYSSA

You're going to hang it in *your* house.

HOLDEN
(laughs)

Yeah, right.

ALYSSA

I'm serious.

HOLDEN *stares at her.*

HOLDEN

Why?

ALYSSA

Because it's captured the moment. It'll be a constant reminder—
not just of tonight, but of our introduction, the building of our
friendship, everything. Make no mistake about it, my friend—it's
a gift to you, from me, so you'll always remember us.

HOLDEN *stares ahead. Then he swerves the wheel to the right.*

EXT: ROADSIDE. NIGHT

The car pulls to the side of the road. The rain is a bit heavier now.

INT: CAR. NIGHT

HOLDEN *throws the car into park.*

ALYSSA

Why are we stopping?

HOLDEN

Because I can't take this.

ALYSSA

Can't take what?

HOLDEN

I love you.

ALYSSA
(beat)

You love me.

HOLDEN

I love you. And not in a friendly way, although I think we're great
friends. And not in a misplaced affection, puppy-dog way,
although I'm sure that's what you'll call it. And it's not because
you're unattainable. I love you. Very simple, very truly. You're
the epitome of every attribute and quality I've ever looked for in
another person. I know you think of me as just a friend, and
crossing that line is the furthest thing from an option you'd ever
consider. But I had to say it. I can't take this anymore. I can't
stand next to you without wanting to hold you. I can't look into
your eyes without feeling that longing you only read about in
trashy romance novels. I can't talk to you without wanting to
express my love for everything you are. I know this will probably
queer our friendship—no pun intended—but I had to say it,
because I've never felt this before, and I like who I am because
of it. And if bringing it to light means we can't hang out anymore,
then that hurts me. But I couldn't allow another day to go by
without getting it out there, regardless of the outcome, which by
the look on your face is to be the inevitable shoot-down. And I'll
accept that. But I know some part of you is hesitating for a
moment, and if there is a moment of hesitation, that means you
feel something too. All I ask is that you not dismiss that—at least
for ten seconds—and try to dwell in it. Alyssa, there isn't another

soul on this fucking planet who's ever made me half the person I am when I'm with you, and I would risk this friendship for the chance to take it to the next plateau. Because it's there between you and me. You can't deny that. And even if we never speak again after tonight, please know that I'm forever changed because of who you are and what you've meant to me, which—while I do appreciate it—I'd never need a painting of birds bought at a diner to remind me of.

HOLDEN *stares at* ALYSSA. *She stares back. Then she gets out of the car.*

> HOLDEN
> Was it something I said?

EXT: ROADSIDE. NIGHT

HOLDEN *gets out of the car. It's raining pretty hard now.* ALYSSA *is hitching up the road.* HOLDEN *reaches her.*

> HOLDEN
> What are you doing?

> ALYSSA
> Get back in the car and get out of here.

> HOLDEN
> You're going to hitch to New York?

> ALYSSA
> Yep.

> HOLDEN
> Aren't you at least going to comment?

> ALYSSA
> Here's my comment: Fuck you.

> HOLDEN
> Why?

> ALYSSA
> That was so unfair. You know how unfair that was.

HOLDEN

It's unfair that I'm in love with you?

ALYSSA

No, it's unfortunate that you're in love with me. It's unfair that
you felt the fucking need to unburden your soul about it. Do you
remember for a fucking second who I am?

HOLDEN

So? People change.

ALYSSA

Oh, it's that simple? You fall in love with me and want a romantic
relationship, nothing changes for you with the exception of
feeling hunky-dory all the time. But what about me? It's not that
simple, is it? I can't just get into a relationship with you without
throwing my whole fucking world into upheaval!

HOLDEN

But that's every relationship! There's always going to be a period
of adjustment.

ALYSSA

Period of adjustment?!?
(hitting him)
THERE'S NO ''PERIOD OF ADJUSTMENT,'' HOLDEN! I'M
FUCKING GAY! THAT'S WHO I AM! AND YOU ASSUME I
CAN TURN ALL THAT AROUND JUST BECAUSE YOU'VE
GOT A FUCKING CRUSH?

HOLDEN

If this is a crush . . . then I don't know if I could take the real
thing if it ever happens.

She looks at him, rain drenching the pair. She shakes her head ruefully.

ALYSSA

Go home, Holden.

*She walks away. HOLDEN stands there, at a loss. Then he turns and
heads back to his car. As he reaches the door and turns to look back at
her, ALYSSA pounces on him, grabs his face, and locks lips with him, big
time. He drops his keys and embraces her.*

And there they stand, by the side of the road, drenched. Kissing.

EXT: STUDIO. DAY

BANKY *carries a bag in one arm and pulls out his keys with the other.
He jams them into the lock, opening the door. He picks up the mail on the
floor.*

INT: STUDIO. DAY

*He closes the door behind him and shuffles to the kitchenette, passing by
the blanket-covered, slumbering forms of* HOLDEN *and* ALYSSA, *who
are out cold in each other's arms. The place looks a mess—like a couple
of people were engaged in some tremendous fucking.* BANKY *is
oblivious. He sets the bag down on the counter and pulls out a chocolate
milk. He opens it, sticks a straw into the top and begins sipping and sifting
through the mail. He comes to mail that's* HOLDEN'S *and tosses it onto
the couch, near* HOLDEN'S *head. He looks down at the sleeping couple,
then back at the mail for a couple of beats. Then he freezes. He looks
down again, and drops his jaw and his carton of chocolate milk. It hits
the floor with a pop.* HOLDEN *and* ALYSSA *shoot straight up, eyes
struggling to focus. They look at each other, then at the flabbergasted*
BANKY. BANKY *blinks. Then he shuffles toward the door again and lets
himself out.*

> ALYSSA
> *(off* HOLDEN'S *reaction)*
> I take it that's not good.

> HOLDEN
> *(getting up)*
> Stay here.
> *(kisses her)*
> I'll be right back.

EXT: STREET. DAY

BANKY *sits on a curb, staring into the distance.* HOLDEN *saunters up
and sits beside him. He follows* BANKY'S *gaze.*

> BANKY
> Catholic schoolgirls.

*Across the street, the Catholic high school is letting out. Teenage girls
clad in uniforms and tight sweaters smoke, frolic, wait for their bus.*

BANKY

The uniform is what does it for me. I wish I'd have went with
more Catholic schoolgirls when I was a kid. As it stands, I have
no ''. . . and then she unzipped her jumper . . .'' stories.

HOLDEN

You looked weirded out back there.

BANKY

That's my couch you were fucking on.

HOLDEN

Sorry.

BANKY

I wanted to watch some TV. Hard to do when your best friend's
wrapped around a naked rug-muncher on your couch.

HOLDEN

She had boxers on.

BANKY *shoots him a glare. He goes back to staring at the OC girls.*

BANKY

This is all going to end badly.

HOLDEN

You don't know that.

BANKY

I know you. You're way too conservative for that girl. She's been
around and seen things we've only read about in books.

HOLDEN

But we have read about them. So we're prepared.

BANKY

There's no ''we'' here. You're going to have to go through this
alone. And it's one thing to read about shit, and something
different when you're forced to deal with it on a regular basis.
When you guys are walking in the mall and both your heads turn
at a really nice-looking chick, it's going to eat you up inside.
You'll spend most of your time wondering when the other shoe's

going to drop. Because for you, this isn't about cool, weird sex stuff. It's about love.

HOLDEN

Maybe it is for her as well.

BANKY

Somehow I doubt it.

HOLDEN

Everyone's not out to get someone in life, Bank.

BANKY

Everybody has an agenda. Everyone.

HOLDEN

Yourself?

BANKY

My agenda is to watch your back.

HOLDEN

To what end?

BANKY

To ensure that all this time we've spent together, building something, wasn't wasted.

HOLDEN

She's not going to ruin the comic.

BANKY

I wasn't talking about the comic.
(gets up)
I'm going to get a bagel. Clean off my fucking couch so I can watch TV.

BANKY *walks away.* HOLDEN *shakes his head.*

INT: ALYSSA'S LIVING ROOM. NIGHT

An all-girl gathering. TORY, NICA, DALIA, *and* JANE *help* ALYSSA *finish an issue of* Idiosyncratic Routine. TORY *letters a page.* NICA *and*

DALIA *lay out the artwork.* DALIA *drinks wine.* ALYSSA *paints the cover.*

DALIA

From what I understand, when you sign with a publisher, someone else does all this work for you, and you just sit back and collect.

ALYSSA

And miss these last-minute cram sessions with my nearest and dearest? Never.

TORY

I don't know what she's bitching about. All she's done since we got here is pound Merlot.

DALIA

I'm sorry—weren't you the one who misspelled ''receipt'' on page eighteen? Yeah, you're a real help.

NICA

What I'd like to know is why we're here at all when we haven't seen Princess Funny-Book in a month.

JANE

Yeah, Alyssa, who've you been shacking up with?

ALYSSA

''Shacking up?'' Please.
          (stops painting; smiles wide)
I'm so in love!

Everyone aww's. ALYSSA *buries her face, giggling.*

ALYSSA

I know, I know—I feel like such a goon. But I can't help it—we have such a great time together.

DALIA

Who is it? Don't even tell me it's Ms. Thing from the CD place. I'll kill you.

ALYSSA

It's not her. It's someone you guys don't know.

NICA

That chick you left the restaurant with that night?

ALYSSA

They're not from around here.

TORY

Don't even tell me you met her down the shore!

JANE

Eww! Not a bridge-and-tunnel Jersey dyke!

TORY

With huge hair and acid-washed jeans!

They all cackle. ALYSSA *tries to laugh with them.*

DALIA

Come on, Alyss—Hoboken Hussy or what?

ALYSSA

For your information, they don't have big hair or wear acid wash.
(goes back to painting)
They're from my hometown.

DALIA *stares at* ALYSSA, *suspiciously.*

DALIA

Why are you playing the pronoun game?

ALYSSA

What? What are you talking about? I'm not even.

DALIA

You are. "I met *someone.*" "*We* have a great time." "*They're*
from my hometown." Doesn't this tube of wonderful have a
name?

ALYSSA
(beat)

Holden.

All four girls stare at ALYSSA, *a bit horrified. She stops painting.*

JANE

Oh, Alyssa—no. Not you.

TORY

You're dating a guy?

ALYSSA

He's not like a typical man. He's really sweet to me, and we relate
so well. You guys'd love him, really.

They stare at ALYSSA. *Then* DALIA *gets up.*

DALIA

I've gotta go to the store.

JANE

I'll go with.

They exit. ALYSSA *looks to* TORY *and* NICA.

TORY
                    (pouring wine)
Whelp, here's to both of you.
                    (moves the glass to her lips)
Another one bites the dust.

INT: HOLDEN'S BEDROOM. NIGHT

HOLDEN *and* ALYSSA *lie in each other's arms, moonlight bathing them.
She smokes.*

HOLDEN

Can I ask you something?

ALYSSA

Don't even tell me you want to do it again.

HOLDEN

Why me—you know? Why now?

ALYSSA

Because you were giving me that look, and I got wet . . .

HOLDEN

You know what I'm talking about.

ALYSSA

Why not you?

HOLDEN

I'm a guy. You're attracted to girls.

ALYSSA

I see you've been taking notes. Historically, yes—that's true.

HOLDEN

Then why this?

ALYSSA

I've given that a lot of thought, you know? I mean, now that I'm
being ostracized by my friends, I've had a lot of time to think
about all of this. And what I've come up with is really simple: I
came to this on my terms. I didn't just heed what I was taught,
you know? Men and women should be together, it's the natural
way—that kind of thing. I'm not with you because of what family,
society, life tried to instill in me from day one. The way the world
is—how seldom you meet that one person who gets you—it's so
rare. My parents didn't really have it. There was no example set
for me in the world of male/female relationships. And to cut
oneself off from finding that person—to immediately half your
options by eliminating the possibility of finding that one person
within your own gender . . . that just seemed stupid. So I didn't.
But then you come along. You—the one least likely; I mean, you
were a guy.

HOLDEN

Still am.

ALYSSA

And while I was falling for you, I put a ceiling on that, because
you were a guy. Until I remembered why I opened the door to
women in the first place—to not limit the likelihood of finding
that one person who'd complement me so completely. And so
here we are. I was thorough when I looked for you, and I feel
justified lying in your arms—because I got here on my own terms,

and have no question that there was someplace I didn't look. And that makes all the difference.

She snuggles into him and closes her eyes. HOLDEN *stares at the ceiling.*

> HOLDEN
> Can I at least tell people that all you needed was some serious deep-dicking?

She hits him with her pillow. They kiss, deeply—the calm before the storm.

INT: OFFICE. DAY

HOLDEN *draws. A book is thrown in front of him. He looks up.* BANKY *stands there.*

> BANKY
> Check out page forty-eight.

HOLDEN *looks down at the book. It's the Nineteen Eighty-Eight yearbook from Middletown North. He shakes his head at* BANKY *and flips it open.*

On the page is ALYSSA'S *senior-year photo. Under her name is another name in quotes that says "Finger Cuffs."*

> HOLDEN
> *(looking up)*
> So?

> BANKY
> Did you see the nickname?

> HOLDEN
> "Finger Cuffs."

> BANKY
> And . . . ?

> HOLDEN
> And . . . she had a weird nickname. What's your point?

> BANKY
> Do you know why it's "Finger Cuffs"?

HOLDEN

I suppose you do.

BANKY

I do.

(takes a seat)

You remember Cohee Lundin? Left Hudson and went to North our senior year?

HOLDEN

Yeah.

BANKY

Well, asshole, I ran into him at the stores the other day. God, it's been ages since I've seen him. We had a great conversation. I mentioned that you were dating Alyssa.

HOLDEN

(barely tolerating it)

Did you?

BANKY

Yeah. Funny thing is, you know what he said . . .

Cut to COHEE LUNDIN, *in the parking lot of Quick Stop, addressing the camera.*

COHEE

Alyssa Jones? Shit, I know Alyssa Jones. I mean, I *know* Alyssa Jones, you know what I'm saying? Me and Rick Derris used to hang out with her for a while, right? Just hanging around her house after school, 'cuz her parents were like never home, and shit. And one day, Rick just whips it out, and starts rubbing it on her leg and shit; chasing her around the living room—I was dying. But you know what the crazy bitch did? She fucking drops to her knees, and just starts sucking him off right in front of me! Like I wasn't even there, man! I almost died! But that's not the fucked-up part—the fucked-up part was Rick, man—right in the middle of it, he turns to me and he's pointing at her and he says, "Cohee." Just like that—"Cohee." So I'm like I'll give it a shot. And I start pulling her pants down all slow, 'cuz I figure any second she's gonna turn around and belt me in the mouth, right? But yo, check this shit out—she's all into it, man! She don't try to stop me or nothing! She's all wet and shit, and I just went to work, know what I'm saying? Me and Rick are going to town on this crazy bitch, and she's just loving it, all moaning and shit! It was fucked up! So Rick's the one that came up with the nickname—cuz that day, she had us locked in tight from both sides—like a pair of goddamn Chinese finger cuffs!

Back in the office, HOLDEN *stares at* BANKY.

HOLDEN

He's full of shit.

BANKY

Cohee's a lot of things, all right, but an exaggerator he's not. The dude's Catholic.

HOLDEN

She's never even been with a guy.

BANKY

That's what she says. But I say her on her hands and knees getting filled out like an application constitutes ''being with a guy.''

HOLDEN

He's pulling your chain. And the fact that you even bought it for a second makes you look like an idiot.

BANKY

I'm getting your back, asshole! People don't forget shit like ''Finger Cuffs.'' And if it got out that she's queer as well, how do you think it's going to make you look?

HOLDEN

I give a shit what people think.

BANKY

All right, forget about that; what if she's carrying a disease?

HOLDEN
(grabs his coat)
You're such a fucking asshole.

BANKY

What? Oh, it's not possible that she's all crudded up? Cohee I can vouch for as clean—the dude never got laid in high school. But Derris? He's an arch-fucking Bushman! Name me one chick in our senior class that Rick Derris *didn't* nail, for Christ's sake!

HOLDEN

Would you let this go? I'm telling you—she's never even been with a guy, let alone those two zeroes.

BANKY

And I'm telling you, the bitch could be a bigger fucking germ farm than that monkey in *Outbreak!*

HOLDEN *grabs* BANKY *and pins him against the wall.*

HOLDEN

Would you let it go? Do you hear me? I'm tired of this shit! She's my goddamn girlfriend, do you understand? Show her a little fucking respect! And if you ever even so much as mention that Alyssa looks a little peaked from now on, I'll put your fucking teeth down your throat!

He releases BANKY. BANKY *brushes himself off.*

BANKY

Maybe I'll put *your* fucking teeth down *your* throat.

HOLDEN
(*walking out*)
Yeah. Maybe.

BANKY *runs to the open door.*

BANKY
(*calling after him*)
I've been working out, you know!
(*no response*)
You better be ready to make that deal!

The downstairs door slams. BANKY *makes a muscle, then feels it.*

INT: TOWER RECORDS. DAY

HOLDEN *and* HOOPER *peruse laser discs.*

HOOPER

Where's that bitch partner of yours been?

HOLDEN

Sulking. He's having a real problem with this Alyssa thing.

HOOPER

I think it's more like Banky's having a problem with all things
not hetero right about now. And I'm just another paradigm of said
aberration.

HOLDEN

Banky does not hate gays, you know that.

HOOPER

But I do think he is a bit homophobic. And this latest episode
between you and Ms. Thing has tapped into that. In his warped
perception, he lost you to the dark side—which is she.

HOLDEN

You make it sound like me and him were dating.

HOOPER

Don't kid yourself—that boy loves you in a way that he's not
ready to deal with.

HOLDEN
(beat)
He's been digging up dirt on Alyssa.

HOOPER

And just what has Mr. Angela Lansbury uncovered about your
lady fair?

HOLDEN

He heard some bullshit story that she took on two guys.

HOOPER

Really? Well then he's barking up the wrong tree if he wants to
split you up, isn't he? He's not going to make you see the error
of your ways by pointing out how truly gay she's not.
(holds up a disc)
This one?

                    HOLDEN
Have it.
                    (beat)
Actually, it's kind of gotten to me.

                    HOOPER
How so?

                    HOLDEN
Banky's not known for believing misinformation. He's got a
pretty good bullshit detector.

                    HOOPER
So, what if it *is* true? Would that bother you?

                    HOLDEN
Sex with multiple partners?

HOOPER *lets out a faux-shock shriek.*

                    HOLDEN
At the same time.

Again, even louder, hands slapped against his chest.

                    HOLDEN
Thanks for being so comforting.

                    HOOPER
So what do you care?

                    HOLDEN
Well, that's the thing, isn't it? I shouldn't . . . but it gets to me.

                    HOOPER
Kind of gal Alyssa is, you don't think she's been in the middle of
an *all-girl* group-grope?

                    HOLDEN
You see—that doesn't bother me. But the thought of her and guys
. . . Uh!

HOOPER

Oh Holden, I beg you—please don't drop fifty stories in my
opinion of you by falling prey to that latest of trendy beasts.

HOLDEN

Which is?

HOOPER

Lesbian chic. It's oh-so acceptable to be a gay girl nowadays.
People think it's cute, because they've got this fool picture in their
heads about lipstick lesbians—like they all resemble Alyssa—
while most of them look more like you.

HOLDEN

Do I detect a little intersubculture cattiness?

HOOPER

Gay or straight—ugly's still ugly. And most of those boys are
scarey.

HOLDEN

I thought you fags were supposed to be all supersupportive of one
another.

HOOPER

Screw that "all for one" shit. I gotta deal with being the minority
in the minority of the minority, and nobody's supporting my ass?
While the whole of society is fawning over girls-on-girls, here I
sit—a reviled gay man. And to top that off, I'm a gay black
man—notoriously the most swishy of the bunch.

HOLDEN

Three strikes.

HOOPER

Hey, hey! There's a line.

A young BLACK KID *approaches* HOOPER, *holding a comic book.*

KID

Are you Hooper X?

HOOPER
(in militant mode)
A-salaam Alaikum, little brother.

KID

Could you sign my comic?

HOOPER
(signs comic; nods to HOLDEN*)*
See that man there? He's the devil, you understand? Never take
your eye off the Man. Our people took their eyes off him one
time, and he had us in chains in two shakes of his snake's tail.

The KID *offers* HOLDEN *an angry look.* HOOPER *gives him back his
comic.*

HOOPER

Fight the power, little ''G.''

KID

Word is bond.

The KID *leaves.* HOOPER *slips back into his real voice.*

HOOPER

Look at what I have to resort to for professional respect. What is
it about gay men that terrifies the rest of the world?
(shakes his head)
As for this hang-up with Alyssa's past, maybe what's really
bothering you is that your fragile fantasy might not be true.

HOLDEN

What do you mean?

HOOPER

Holden—don't even try to come off like you don't know what
I'm saying. Men need to believe that they're Marco fucking Polo
when it comes to sex—like they're the only ones who've ever
explored new territory. And it's hard not to let them believe it. I
let my boys run with it for a while—feed them some of that ''I've
never done *this* before . . .'' bullshit, and let 'em labor under the
delusion that they rockin' my world, until I can't stand them
anymore. Then I hit 'em with the truth. It's a sick game. The

world would be a better place if people would just accept that there's nothing new under the sun, and everything you can do with a person has probably been done long before you got there.

HOLDEN

I can accept that.

HOOPER

Honey, that almost sounded convincing. Do yourself a favor—just ask her about her past, point blank. Get it out of the way, before it gets too big for both ya'll to move.
                    (spotting something OC)
Oooh! *Myra Breckinridge!*

HOOPER *trots off.* HOLDEN *glances at the disc in his hands. Pictured on it are two gorgeous chicks, barely clad, making out. The title is Men Suck . . . and so Do Girls—All XXX Action.*

INT: HOCKEY RINK. NIGHT

On the ice, two teams clash, chasing the puck up and back, checking galore. In the bleachers, amid a slew of fans, ALYSSA *watches the game with a large degree of enjoyment. Sitting beside her,* HOLDEN *doesn't seem to share her enthusiasm.*

ALYSSA

Since most of these people are rooting for the hometeam, I'm going to cheer for the visitors. I'm a big visitors fan—especially the kind that make coffee for you in the morning before they go.
                    (smiles at HOLDEN; *no response)*
That was a joke. A little wacky word play?

HOLDEN

What do you mean, ''visitors''?

ALYSSA

Was I being too obscure? The kind that—until recently—had no dicks and would spend the night.

HOLDEN

So that was until recently?

ALYSSA

Uh, yeah.

(shouting; to ice)

Hey—foul! Foul! He was traveling or something!

HOLDEN

So nobody but me has stayed the night at your place since we got
together?

ALYSSA

(beat)

Something on your mind, Holden?

HOLDEN

No, I was just wondering.

ALYSSA

If I've been ''faithful'' or something?

HOLDEN

Look, I was just asking.

ALYSSA

(touches his face)

Oh, sweetie. I only have eyes for you.

(to ice)

CALL THAT FUCKING SHIT, REF! THE GUY ON THE
SKATES TOTALLY SHOVED ONE OF MY GUYS!

(to Holden)

I told you I was great at sporting events. Imagine what a bitch I
could be if I knew what was going on?

*On the ice, things heat up between two opposing PLAYERS. One snatches
the puck away from the other and skates off. The other PLAYER gives
chase. ALYSSA'S very into the game. HOLDEN shakes his head.*

HOLDEN

That'd make Banky half right.

ALYSSA

About what?

HOLDEN

He said all the girls from North were bitches and sluts.

ALYSSA

Really. I'm sorry—you two left high school behind how many
years ago?
(grabs his face and kisses his cheek)
Can I put some of my books in your locker?
(goes back to watching game)

HOLDEN
(under his breath)
How about your yearbook.

On the ice, the PLAYER giving chase slashes the PLAYER with the puck.
ALYSSA jumps to her feet.

ALYSSA
(to ice)
IF YOU DON'T START USING THAT WHISTLE, I'M
GONNA JAM IT STRAIGHT UP YOUR ASS!!
(to guy next to her)
Right?

HOLDEN
What's with ''Finger Cuffs''?

ALYSSA
(sitting back down)
''Finger Cuffs''?

HOLDEN
Yeah. In your senior yearbook, your nickname was ''Finger
Cuffs.'' What is that?

ALYSSA
It was? Shit, damned if I can remember. I'd look it up, but I threw
all that shit out years ago.
(beat)
Where'd you see a North yearbook?

HOLDEN
Do you know a guy named Rick Derris?

On the ice, the PLAYERS skid into the corner where PLAYER ONE
checks PLAYER TWO into the boards, hard. PLAYER TWO scrambles
to his feet and throws down his gloves.

The crowd around ALYSSA and HOLDEN goes wild.

ALYSSA

Rick Derris? Sure. We used to hang out in high school.

(to ice)

PUNCH HIM IN THE FUCKING NECK, NUMBER TWELVE!!

HOLDEN

Did you go out with him or something?

ALYSSA

(eyes on the ice)

Date Rick Derris? No. We just hung out a lot.

HOLDEN

Just . . . you and Rick?

ALYSSA

No. Me, Rick, and . . . um . . . what was that guy's name . . . ?

HOLDEN

Cohee?

ALYSSA

Yeah! Cohee—Cohee Lundin. God, I haven't thought about that name in years.

On the ice, the PLAYERS *square off.* PLAYER TWO *pulls* PLAYER ONE'S *helmet off and punches him in the face.* HOLDEN *looks as if he'd like to do the same to his companion.* ALYSSA'S *into the game.*

ALYSSA

I remember those guys'd come over almost everyday after school. They'd bug my sisters, look for porno tapes in my dad's closet, raid our fridge. They really took advantage of my parents never being home.

On the ice, PLAYER TWO *yanks at* PLAYER ONE'S *jersey and gut-punches him.* ALYSSA *seems oblivious of* HOLDEN'S *anger, so enthralled with the action is she.*

ALYSSA

(starts laughing)

This one day . . . Rick pulled out his dick and chased me around the house with it! Right in front of Cohee! I couldn't believe it!

Guys are weird—I thought the whole size hang-up made you all terrified to show your dicks to each other?

On the ice, PLAYER ONE *staggers a bit, then quickly rights his jersey and lunges at* PLAYER TWO, *landing a barrage of his own punches. Blood sprays across the ice.*

HOLDEN'S *face is* really *sour looking.* ALYSSA'S *still in the game.*

> HOLDEN
> Rick pulled his dick out? Really? What'd you do?

> ALYSSA
> *(looks him dead in the eye)*
> I blew him while Cohee fucked me.

On the ice, PLAYER ONE *delivers the kill shot, slamming his fist into* PLAYER TWO'S *nose. The blood shoots out like a geyser, and* TWO *goes down hard.*

HOLDEN *stares at* ALYSSA, *flabbergasted. The crowd around them stares not at the fight on the ice, but the fight in their midst, shocked.* ALYSSA *fumes.*

> HOLDEN
> Excuse me?

> ALYSSA
> That's what you wanted to hear, isn't it? Isn't that what this little cross-examination of yours is about? Well, try not to be so obvious about it next time; there are subtler ways of badgering a witness.
> *(to* BYSTANDER*)*
> Am I right?

> BYSTANDER
> *(to* HOLDEN*)*
> Jeez, even I knew what you were getting at.

> ALYSSA
> *(gathering her stuff)*
> If you wanted some background information on me, all you had to do was ask—I'd have gladly volunteered it. You didn't have to play Hercule fucking Poirot!

She storms away. HOLDEN *chases after her. The* BYSTANDER *watches them go.*

> BYSTANDER
> *(to companion)*
> I told you these were good seats.

EXT: RINK PARKING LOT. NIGHT

ALYSSA *marches quickly, pulling on her coat.* HOLDEN *catches up to her. We track with them out into the parking lot.*

> HOLDEN
> So it's true?

> ALYSSA
> Is that what you want to hear? Is it? Yes, Holden, it's true! In fact, everything you heard or dug up on me was probably true! Yeah, I took on two guys at once! You want to hear some gems you might not have unearthed—I took a twenty-six-year-old guy to my senior prom, and then left halfway through to have sex with him and Gwen Turner in the back of a limo! And the girl who got caught in the shower with Miss Moffit, the gym teacher? That was me! Or how about in college, when I let Shannon Hamilton videotape us having sex—only to find out the next day that he broadcast it on the campus cable station? They're all true—those and so many more! Didn't you know? I'm the queen of urban legend!

> HOLDEN
> How the hell could you do those things?!

> ALYSSA
> Easily! Some of it I did out of stupidity, some of it I did out of what I thought was love, but—good or bad—they were my choices, and I'm not making apologies for them now—not to you or anyone! And how dare you try to lay a guilt trip on me about it—in public, no less! Who the fuck do you think you are, you judgmental prick?

> HOLDEN
> How am I supposed to feel about all of this?

ALYSSA

How are you supposed to feel about it? Feel whatever the fuck you want about it! The only thing that really matters is how you feel about me.

HOLDEN

I don't know how I feel about you now.

ALYSSA

Why? Because I had some sex?

HOLDEN

Some sex?

ALYSSA

Yes, Holden—that's all it was: some sex! Most of it stupid high school sex, for Christ's sake! Like you never had sex in high school!

HOLDEN

There's a world of fucking difference between typical high school sex and getting fucked by two guys at the same time! They fucking used you!

ALYSSA

NO! I used *them*! You don't think I would've let it happen if I hadn't wanted it to, do you?! I was an experimental girl, for

Christ's sake! Maybe you knew early on that your track was from point *A* to *B*—but unlike you, I wasn't given a fucking map at birth, so I tried it all! That is until *we*—that's you and I—got together, and suddenly, I was sated. Can't you take some fucking comfort in that? You turned out to be all I was ever looking for—the missing piece in the big fucking puzzle!
(tries to calm down)
Look, I'm sorry I let you believe that you were the only guy I'd ever been with. I should've been more honest. But it seemed to make you feel special in a way that me telling you over and over again how incredible you are would never get across.

She touches his face. He pulls back. She stares at him, hurt and pissed.

ALYSSA

Do you mean to tell me that while you have zero problem with me sleeping with half the women in New York City you have some sort of half-assed, mealymouthed objection to pubescent antics that took place almost ten years ago? What the fuck is your problem?

HOLDEN'S *eyes are downcast.* ALYSSA *waits for a response.*

HOLDEN

I want us to be something that we can't be.

ALYSSA

And what's that?

HOLDEN
(beat)

A normal couple.

HOLDEN *skulks off.* ALYSSA *stares after him, and then starts kicking and punching a car beside her, finally slumping to the ground. She cries.*

INT: STUDIO. DAWN

HOLDEN *sits on the couch, alone in the morning light, a half-empty bottle of booze and an ashtray full of smoked butts in front of him. The door opens and* BANKY *enters. He stands there, sizing up* HOLDEN'S *mood.*

BANKY

The girl?

HOLDEN *nods.* BANKY *nods back. He stands there for a beat. Then he
sits beside* HOLDEN. *He opens his arms.* HOLDEN *shifts into his friend's
embrace and begins crying on his shoulder.* BANKY *pats his back. Pull
back on a man in pain and the comfort of a friend.*

INT: DINER. NIGHT

HOLDEN *sits alone at a booth.*

(OC) VOICE

Yo, look at this morose motherfucker here . . .

HOLDEN *looks up.* JAY *and* SILENT BOB *stand above him.*

JAY

Smells like somebody shit in his cereal.

HOLDEN *offers a half-smile. The pair slide into the booth.*

HOLDEN

What took you guys so long? Were you at the mall again or
something?

JAY

Bitch, don't even start. We stopped that shit years ago. Toss the
salad.

HOLDEN *pulls an envelope out of his jacket and tosses it to* JAY. JAY
opens it and pulls out a thick wad of bills, along with the latest issue of
Bluntman and Chronic.

JAY

Man, this likeness rights shit is more profitable than selling
smoke.

HOLDEN

How'd a dirt merchant like you ever learn about likeness rights?

JAY
(hands envelope to Silent Bob)
We deal to a lot of lawyers. Speaking of which . . .
(pulls out a dime bag)
Little signing bonus and shit?

HOLDEN
I'll pass. Take a look at the issue.

SILENT BOB *thumbs through the comic.* JAY *looks over his shoulder, as he begins rolling a joint.*

JAY
Yeah, yeah, yeah. When you gonna get some pussy in that book, man? Throw some supervillain in with big fucking tits that shoot milk or something, and I just suck her dry, bust some moves on her . . .
(demonstrates)
. . . and then she has to fuck me.
(SILENT BOB hits him)
Fuck us.

HOLDEN
I'll see what I can do.

A WAITRESS *joins them.*

WAITRESS
What can I get you?

HOLDEN
Nothing, thanks.

JAY
Yo, Flo, tell Mel to whip me up a toasted bagel and cream cheese.
(to SILENT BOB*)*
You want one too?
(SILENT BOB nods)
Make that two. And kiss my grits. Noonch.
(the WAITRESS *leaves; to* HOLDEN*)*
D'jever watch *Alice*? That show's good as hell.
(continues rolling)
So why the long face, Horse? Banky on the rag?

HOLDEN

I'm just having some girl trouble.

JAY

Bitch pressing charges? I get that a lot.

HOLDEN

No. I'm just at a point where I don't know what to do.

JAY

Kick her to the curb. Girls get to be too much trouble, there's
always the "band of the hand."

HOLDEN

Can't do it, G. I'm in love.

JAY

Ah, there ain't no such thing. You gotta boil it all down to the
essentials. It's like Cube says—life ain't nothing but bitches and
money.

HOLDEN

Just what I needed—advice from the 'hood.

JAY

Who is this girl?

HOLDEN

I don't think you know her.

JAY

Come on man—I'm people who know people.

HOLDEN

You sound like Barbra Streisand.

JAY

That's 'cause I got this tubby bitch playing her greatest hits tape
in my ear all the time. You should see him: she starts singing
"You Don't Bring Me Flowers," this faggot starts crying like a
little girl with a skinned knee and shit. It's embarrassing. I got the
only muscle in the world with a weakness for ballads.

> (*to* SILENT BOB)

You big fucking softie.

> (*to* HOLDEN)

So what's this skirt's name?

HOLDEN

I'm telling you, you don't know her.

JAY

I ain't playing, man. Tell me her name, Mysterio.

HOLDEN

Alyssa Jones.

JAY

Finger Cuffs?

HOLDEN *rubs his eyes.*

JAY

Holy fucking shit—Finger Cuffs? You're dating Finger Cuffs, you silly sonovabitch? Wait a minute—I thought she was all gay and shit?

HOLDEN

She is. Or was. I don't know.

The WAITRESS *returns with the order.*

JAY

And you go out with her? Shit, man—you're a lucky fuck. She ever bring other chicks to bed with you, get a little of that filet o'fish sammich going on?

The WAITRESS *stares wide-eyed and offended at* JAY.

JAY

> (*off* WAITRESS'S *look*)

Yeah—you know what I'm talking about, baby.

> (WAITRESS *leaves; to* HOLDEN)

So—four tits, or what?

HOLDEN

It's not like that.

What's it like then?

Right now?
(beat)
I don't know. I love her. But she has a past.

I'll say. Stuffin' two guys, eating chicks out. Yo—I heard one
time, she had this dog . . .

Eat your fucking bagel already and shut up!

(to SILENT BOB)
Look at this touchy motherfucker right here.
(to HOLDEN)
So, if you're all in love and shit, what's the problem?

The problem is shit like that. It was one thing when it was just
girls—that was weird enough. But now you throw guys into the
mix—two guys at once, no less. All that experience . . . What am
I supposed to think?

You think good, you ninny shithead; because now she'll be all
true blue and shit. Bitch tasted life, yo. Now she's settlin' for your
boring, funny-book-makin' ass.

Settling. That's comforting, Jay. Thanks.

That's what I'm here for.

I'm just having a problem with all of it. I can't get it out of my
head, these visuals of her doing all this shit. And I don't know
why I can't let it go. Because I'm crazy about her, you know? I
look at this girl, I see kids. I see grandkids.

                                    JAY
     You're scaring me.

                                 HOLDEN
     I'm scaring myself. Because I think so much of her, and then I
     can't get shit like "Finger Cuffs" out of my head.
                            (shakes his head)
     I don't know what I'm doing.

     HOLDEN *looks out the window.* JAY *continues to roll his joint. There's
     silence. Then . . .*

                                    BOB
     You're chasing Amy.

     HOLDEN'S *head snaps forward. He stares, wide-eyed at* SILENT BOB.

                                 HOLDEN
     What . . . what did you say?

                                    BOB
     You're chasing Amy.

     HOLDEN *stares, shocked. He looks to* JAY, *who's still rolling his joint.*

                                    JAY
     What do you look so shocked for? He does this all the time. Fat
     bastard thinks just because he never says anything, that it'll have
     some huge impact when he does open his fucking mouth.

                                    BOB
     Why don't you shut up? Jesus! Always yap, yap, yapping all the
     time. Give me a fucking headache.
                               (to HOLDEN*)*
     I went through something like what you're talking about. Couple
     years ago, with this chick named Amy.

                                    JAY
     When?

                                    BOB
     A couple of years ago.

JAY

What'd she "live in Canada" or something? Why don't I
remember this?

BOB

Bitch, what you don't know about me I can just about squeeze
into the Grand fucking Canyon. Did you know I always wanted
to be a dancer in Vegas?

JAY *and* HOLDEN *look at him.* SILENT BOB *busts a move with his
hands.*

BOB

Hunhh? Bet you didn't even know that shit, did you?

JAY

Just tell your fucking story so we can get out of here and smoke
this.

BOB
(to HOLDEN*)*

So there's me and Amy, and we're all inseparable, right? Just big
time in love. And then about four months down the road, the idiot
gear kicks in, and I ask about the ex-boyfriend—which, as we all
know, is a really dumb move. But you know how it is—you don't
want to know, but you just *have* to . . . stupid guy bullshit.
Anyway, she starts telling me all about him—how they fell in
love, how they dated for a couple of years, how they lived
together, her mother likes me better, blah, blah, blah—and I'm
okay. But then she drops the bomb on me, and the bomb is this:
It seems that a couple times, while they were going out, he
brought some people to bed with them—menage à trois, I believe
it's called. Now this just blows my mind. I mean, I'm not used to
that sort of thing, right? I was raised Catholic, for God's sake.

JAY

Saint Shithead.

SILENT BOB *backhands him.* JAY *raises his fist as if to strike.*

BOB

Do something.
(to HOLDEN*)*

So I get weirded out, and just start blasting her, right? I don't
know how to deal with what I'm feeling. But I figure the best way

is if I call her a slut and tell her that she was used. I mean, I'm
out for blood. I want to hurt this girl now. And I'm like ''What
the fuck is your problem?'' and she's calmly telling me that it
was that time, in that place, and she didn't do anything wrong, so
she's not gonna apologize. And I'm like ''Oh really?'' That's
when I look her straight in the eye and tell her it's over. I walk.

JAY

Fucking A.

BOB

No, idiot. It was a mistake. I wasn't disgusted with her, I was
afraid. At that moment, I felt small—like I'd lacked experience,
like I'd never be on her level or never be enough for her or
something. And what I didn't get was that she didn't care. She
wasn't looking for that guy anymore. She was looking for me.
But by the time I realized this, it was too late, you know. She'd
moved on, and all I had to show for it was some foolish pride,
which then gave way to regret. She was the girl, I know that now.
But I pushed her away . . .

Everyone's silent. SILENT BOB *lights a cigarette.*

BOB

So I've spent every day since then chasing Amy . . .
    (takes a drag from his smoke)
So to speak.

They sit there for a beat. JAY *pockets the rest of his dime bag.*

                              JAY
Enough of this fucking melodrama. My advice—forget her, dude.
There's one bitch in the world. One bitch, with many faces.
                     (to SILENT BOB*)*
Get up, tons of fun.
                      (to HOLDEN*)*
We gotta book. We're catching a bus to Chi-town.

                            HOLDEN
What's there?

                              JAY
Business, yo. How many more of those phat envelopes do we got
coming to us?

                            HOLDEN
I don't know. I don't know if the book's going to be around much
longer.

                              JAY
Yeah? Good. I'll be glad as shit when it's gone.

                            HOLDEN
Are you kidding me? There's millions of people out there that'd
love to see themselves in a comic book.

                              JAY
I know. I spend every fucking waking hour with one of them.
Don't get me wrong—I love how you draw us and shit. But it
ain't like us at all—all slap-sticky and shit—running around like
a couple of dickheads, saying . . .
                     (to SILENT BOB*)*
What's that shit he got us saying?

                             BOB
Snootchie-bootchies.

                              JAY
"Snootchie-bootchies." Who the fuck talks like that? That is
fucking baby talk.
                     (slaps his hand)

It's a big world, G—but we're bound to run into you again. Until then—keep your unit on you.

                    HOLDEN
I'll try.

                    BOB
Do, or do not—there is no try.

                    JAY
                 (slaps him)
Knock it off! We got a bus to catch.
                 (under his breath)
Jedi bitch.

Exit JAY and SILENT BOB. HOLDEN remains in the booth, thinking.

EXT: RIVERFRONT PARK. DAY

HOLDEN sits in the park that he and ALYSSA walked through. He's staring at ALYSSA'S yearbook picture. He closes the book and sighs. Then, an idea hits him. He jumps up and dashes out of the park.

INT: STUDIO. NIGHT

BANKY and ALYSSA sit on the couch. HOLDEN paces in front of them.

                    HOLDEN
I know you're wondering why I asked you both here tonight, at the same time, knowing that we have shit to settle between us, separately.

                    BANKY
I just figured you wanted to kill two birds with one stone by telling her to fuck off with me here so you didn't have to go through the story again later on.

                    ALYSSA
Fuck you.

                    BANKY
Not even if you let me videotape it.

HOLDEN

Enough.

(they both look at him)

I've been going through things, over and over. And I dissected it all and looked at it a thousand different ways. Banky—there's tension between us for the first time in our lives. You hate me dating Alyssa, and you want me to sign off on this cartoon thing.

BANKY

How perceptive.

HOLDEN

Alyssa—you and I hit a wall, because I don't know how to deal with . . . your past, I guess.

BANKY

That's a nice way of putting it. I'd have said the whole double-stuff thing . . .

HOLDEN

(right in his face)

I'm only going to say this once: Shut up.

(back to pacing)

Now—I know I'm to blame one way or the other on both accounts. With you, Alyssa—it's because I feel inadequate. Because you've had so much experience, had such a big life; and my life's been pretty small in comparison.

ALYSSA

That doesn't matter to me . . .

HOLDEN

Please. I have to get through this.

(beat)

And with you, Banky—I know why you're having such a hard time with Alyssa, and it's something that's been obvious forever, but I guess I just didn't acknowledge it.

(takes a deep breath)

You're in love with me.

BANKY

(makes a face; beat)

What?

HOLDEN

You're attracted to me. Just as, in a way, I'm attracted to you. I mean, it makes sense—we've been together so long, we have so much in common . . .

BANKY
(getting up)
Well, I've gotta get going. Gotta catch the last few minutes of *Little House,* so I'll be . . .

HOLDEN *grabs him, kisses him full on the lips, and pushes him back onto the couch. ALYSSA reacts. BANKY—wide-eyed and speechless—looks away.*

HOLDEN

It's something you're going to have to deal with, Bank. It would explain your homophobia, your jealousy of Alyssa, your sense of humor . . .

BANKY

Just 'cause a guy's got a predilection toward dick jokes . . .

HOLDEN

Bank. Stop. Deal with it. You'll feel much better.

He grabs a chair from the side of the room.

HOLDEN

Now—at this point, you may be asking yourself the question that I've been going over and over in my head for the last few weeks: What does one have to do with the other?

ALYSSA'S *face drops. She subtly shakes her head.*

ALYSSA
(under her breath)
Don't.

HOLDEN

And when I did some serious soul searching, it came at me from out of nowhere, and suddenly it all made sense—a calm came over me. I know what we have to do. And then you—Banky, you—Alyssa, and I—all of us . . . can finally be . . . all right.

ALYSSA
(again, under her breath)
Please don't say it.

HOLDEN
(sits in the chair; takes a long beat)
We've all got to have sex together.

The room is silent. BANKY'S eyes nearly bug. ALYSSA'S head drops.

HOLDEN
Don't you see? That would take care of everything. Alyssa—I
wouldn't feel inadequate or too conservative anymore. I'll have
done something on par with all the experience you've had. And
it'll be with you, which'll make it that much more powerful. And
Banky—you can take that leap that everyone else but you sees
that you should take. And it'll be okay, because it'll be with
me—your best friend for years. We've been everything to each
other but intimates. And now, we'll have been through that
together too. And it won't have to be a total leap for you, because
a woman will be involved. And when it's over, all that hostility
and aggression you feel toward Alyssa will be gone. Because
you'll have shared in something beautiful with the woman I love.
It'll be cathartic. A true communion. I need this. For me, for both
of you . . . for all of our sakes. This will keep us together.
(beat)
What do you say?

*BANKY stares forward, wide-eyed. He leans back into the couch and lets
out a huge sigh. Then shrugs.*

BANKY
Sure.

HOLDEN *smiles at his friend. Then he looks at* ALYSSA.

HOLDEN
You know I need this. You know it'll help.

ALYSSA *looks at him, sadly.*

ALYSSA
No.

HOLDEN *reacts, shocked.* BANKY *lets out a sigh of relief.*

BANKY

Thank Christ.

ALYSSA *and* HOLDEN *react.* BANKY *looks at them sheepishly.*

BANKY

Sorry.

HOLDEN
(to Alyssa)
No? I thought you'd be into this.

ALYSSA

You did? What does that say about me?

HOLDEN

But you've done . . . stuff . . . like this. This should be no big deal
for you.

ALYSSA

You don't want this.
(lights her cigarette)
You really don't want this.

HOLDEN

I do want this. This has to happen. Can't you see that? And how
can you not? What does that say about me? You can take it from
two guys whose names you can barely remember, but I ask you
to share an experience like it—where it's about intimacy—and
you say no?

ALYSSA

I can't!

HOLDEN *moves to her side of the couch.*

HOLDEN

You can. I'll be there. And when it's over, we'll be the strongest
we've ever been because we got through this together. And we'll
finally be on the same level together. And there'll be nothing we
can't accomplish.

A tear rolls down her cheek. She looks at him, sadly, and touches his face.

ALYSSA

Oh, Holden.
(trying to compose herself)
That time is over for me. I've been there. I've done it. And I
didn't find what I was looking for in any of it. I found that in
you—in us. Doing this won't help you forget about the things
you're hung up on. It'll create more.

HOLDEN

No it won't. I thought about all of that.

ALYSSA

Yes, it will! Maybe you'll see me differently from then on—
maybe you'll despise me for going along with it, once you're in
the moment. Maybe I'll moan differently, and then you'll resent
Banky and become suspicious of us. Or you'll alienate him
because of it, and then grow to blame and hate me for the
deterioration of your friendship. Or what if—I sincerely doubt it,
but what if—I saw something in Banky that I never saw before,
and fell in love with him and left you? I've been down roads like
this before, many times. I know you feel doing this will broaden
your horizons and give you experience. But I've had those
experiences on my own. I can't accompany you on yours. I'm
past that now.
(touches his face; starts to cry)
Or maybe I just love you too much. And I feel hurt and let down
that you'd want to share me with anyone. Because I would never
want to share you.
(holds it in; gets up)
Regardless. I can't be a part of this.
(beat)
Or you. Not anymore.
(hugs him)
I love you. I always will. Know that.

She releases him, then slaps him.

ALYSSA

But I'm not your fucking whore.

ALYSSA *storms away, stopping briefly to look* BANKY *up and down.*

293

ALYSSA

He's yours again.

She walks out of the studio. The door closes behind her.

BANKY *and* HOLDEN *stand there, silently.* BANKY *quietly heads to his room, leaving* HOLDEN *standing there—alone. Fade to black.*

INT: COMIC BOOK SHOW. DAY

It's one year later. We're at another show, not unlike the one from the opening.

A copy of Bluntman and Chronic *enters the frame. The cover reads "The Death of Chronic," complete with a corresponding drawing.*

BANKY (VO)

Blast from the past.

BANKY *sits at his own signing table. Behind him hangs a banner that reads* BANKY EDWARDS—CREATOR OF BABY DAVE. *A small line is formed in front of him.* He talks with a FAN.

FAN

Do you know how much it's going for these days? One-ten. You signing it will push that up even higher.

BANKY

If you sell it, I want a kickback.
                    (starts signing)

FAN

I don't know if this is true, but I heard once that there was going to be an animated series.

BANKY

There was going to be.

FAN

What happened?

BANKY
                    (off comic)
You're looking at it. No Chronic—no cartoon.

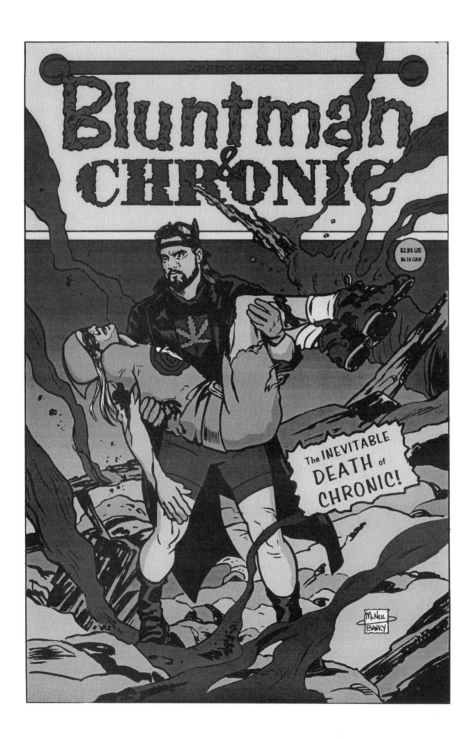

FAN

That sucks, man. That would've been awesome.

BANKY

Tell me about it.

FAN

Is that what happened to you and Holden McNeil? You got into a
fight over the rights or something?

BANKY

It was a little more complicated than that.

FAN

Whatever happened to him?

BANKY

He quit the biz, I guess.

FAN

You guys don't talk anymore?

BANKY
(looks OC)

No. Not really.

BANKY *locks eyes with someone OC. His expression softens.*

HOLDEN *leans against a wall on the far side of the room. He smiles at*
BANKY. *Meanwhile, the* FAN *rambles on.*

(OC) FAN

Yeah—that happened to me once. Me and this guy started a comic
club, and we got in a fight over who looked better in tights—
Elektra or Robin. Anyway, I disbanded the club and just struck
out on my own—kind of like Nomad, you know?

BANKY *smiles back at* HOLDEN—*then sort of nods.*

(OC) FAN

Oh—I'm rambling on now. What I mean to say is that you
probably shouldn't have killed off Chronic.

HOLDEN *holds up a copy of* BANKY'S *new solo comic. He points to it and gives a thumbs up.* BANKY *smiles back at the OC* HOLDEN.

> BANKY
> *(to* FAN; *not looking at him)*
> Guess not. Some doors just shouldn't be opened.

BANKY *looks in another direction, OC. He looks at* HOLDEN *and points to it.*

> (OC) FAN
> Oh—like the "Door to Death" in Baby Dave's *Winter Special.* Which you did on your own.

HOLDEN *looks in the same direction, and then looks back at* BANKY *and nods.*

> (OC) FAN
> See? You don't need that McNeil guy, anyway. You do great work on your own.

BANKY *looks at* HOLDEN *for a beat. Then he brings his pointer fingers together, mimicking* HOLDEN'S *"shared moment" gesture.*

> (OC) FAN
> Look at your linework. Look at all the detail in this douchebag on page eighteen. Look at how you draw a fart and tell me you're not better off without Holden McNeil.

HOLDEN *shrugs slightly, then crosses his fingers—as if to say "hopefully."*

> (OC) FAN
> You were just carrying that guy like a brown-bagged lunch, you know what I'm saying?

BANKY *sort of smiles at the OC* HOLDEN. *Then he offers his own thumbs up—as if to say "good luck."*

> BANKY
> *(to fan, still looking at OC* HOLDEN*)*
> You're so right.

HOLDEN *smiles back, nods, and walks off.*

Yeah—the true fans always are. Well, keep up the good work, man. Love them dick jokes. Love 'em. See ya.

The FAN *leaves, but* BANKY *is watching* HOLDEN *go.*

BANKY
Yeah. Bye.
(shakes it off)
Okay. Who's next?

ALYSSA *sits at a separate signing table, with a line in front of her. A* WOMAN *sits next to her.* ALYSSA *dashes off signatures in the copies of her comic.*

ALYSSA
(to OC departing fan)
Thanks for reading it.

The WOMAN *rolls her eyes.*

WOMAN
I can't believe this place. These people are so weird.

ALYSSA
You wanted to come.

WOMAN
I can't believe you call these people contemporaries. Look at this guy over here with the pointed ears. What's that?

ALYSSA
He's a Vulcan.

WOMAN
A what?

ALYSSA
A Vulcan. Jesus, Potzer. Why don't you take a walk and get us something to drink?

WOMAN

Okay, I will.

The WOMAN heads off. ALYSSA starts rummaging through her bag. A comic book drops on the table in front of her. It's a comic book called Chasing Amy. *She leafs through it, not looking up.*

ALYSSA

Um . . . This isn't one of mine.

(OC) HOLDEN

It's mine.

ALYSSA *looks up sharply.* HOLDEN *stands before her, smiling.*

HOLDEN

I saved you a copy.

ALYSSA

Hi.

HOLDEN

Hi.

ALYSSA
(beat)

How've you been?

HOLDEN

Good. Really good. Yourself?

ALYSSA

Good.
(beat; off her own comic)
New issue's selling like crazy, for some reason.

HOLDEN

Because it's really good. I liked it a lot.

ALYSSA

Thank you.
(off comic)
I haven't even seen this yet. Did it just come out?

HOLDEN

A month ago. I did a really small run. Self-financed. Only about five hundred issues.

ALYSSA

Will I enjoy it?

HOLDEN

You might. It's familiar subject matter.

ALYSSA *leafs through it. Her eyes get somewhat misty.*

ALYSSA

Looks like a very personal story.

HOLDEN

I finally had something personal to say.

They look at each other for a beat.

HOLDEN

I'm going to go. I don't want to hold up the line.

ALYSSA

Yeah. I mean, it can get ugly. I just saw this nun call this small child a cunt-rag.

HOLDEN
(smiles)
Read that, when you have a minute.

ALYSSA

I will.

HOLDEN

I'd like to hear your thoughts about it. If you get a chance, give me a call.

ALYSSA

Okay.

They look at each other for a beat.

HOLDEN

Okay.
(beat)
It was really nice seeing you again.

ALYSSA

It was really nice to see you too.

He walks away.

The WOMAN returns with drinks. She follows ALYSSA'S gaze.

WOMAN

Who was that?

ALYSSA
(distracted)

Hunhh?

WOMAN

Who was that?

HOLDEN *stops at the exit door. He looks back briefly. Then, he's gone.*
ALYSSA *watches him go for another beat, then.*

ALYSSA

Oh. Just some guy I knew.

ALYSSA
(to line)

Next.
(to WOMAN)
So what do you want to do tonight?

And as they fall into conversation, the show goes on.

Miramax Films Presents

A View Askew Production

chasing amy

BEN AFFLECK
JOEY LAUREN ADAMS
JASON LEE
DWIGHT EWELL
and
JASON MEWES

"Bluntman & Chronic/Chasing Amy"
artwork by
MIKE ALLRED

Costume Designer
CHRISTOPHER DEL CORO

Line Producer
DERRICK TSENG

Edited by
KEVIN SMITH
SCOTT MOSIER

Production Designer
ROBERT "RATFACE" HOLTZMAN

Director of Photography
DAVID KLEIN

Music by
DAVID PIRNER

Executive Producer
JOHN PIERSON

Associate Producer
ROBERT HAWK

Produced by
SCOTT MOSIER

Written and Directed by
KEVIN SMITH

cast

[In Order of Appearance]

Fan	**ETHAN SUPLEE**
Holden	**BEN AFFLECK**
Collector	**SCOTT MOSIER**
Banky	**JASON LEE**
Little Kid	**CASEY AFFLECK**
Hooper	**DWIGHT EWELL**
Alyssa	**JOEY LAUREN ADAMS**
Singer	**GUINEVERE TURNER**
Kim	**CARMEN LEE**
Exec. #1	**BRIAN O'HALLORAN**
Exec. #2	**MATT DAMON**
Train Kid	**ALEXANDER GOEBBEL**

Cashier	**TONY TORN**
Dalia	**REBECCA WAXMAN**
Tory	**PARIS PETRICK**
Jane	**WELKER WHITE**
Nica	**KELLI SIMPKINS**
Cohee Lundin	**JOHN WILLYUNG**
Young Black Kid	**TSEMACH WASHINGTON**
Bystander	**ERNIE O'DONNELL**
Jay	**JASON MEWES**
Silent Bob	**KEVIN SMITH**
Waitress	**KRISTIN MOSIER**
Con Woman	**VIRGINIA SMITH**
Production Manager and Production Auditor	**MONICA HAMPTON**
First Assistant Director	**JOHN M. TYSON**
Second Assistant Director	**LINDA KRANTZ**
Camera Operator	**DAVID KLEIN**
First Camera Assistant	**KELLY BALDWIN**
Second Camera Assistant	**MICHELE LEE KIRWAN**
Steadicam Operator	**DAVID KLEIN**
Still Photographer	**LORENZO BEVILAQUA**
Second Unit Director	**DAVID KLEIN**
Art Director	**JIM WILLIAMS**
Set Decorator	**SUSANNAH McCARTHY**
Leadman	**HOWARD CHELDER**
Set Dresser	**JENNIFER COOKE**
Property Master	**AUGUSTA "GUSSY" HOPKINS**
Bluntman & Chronic Action Sequence Artwork	**MATT BRUNDAGE**
	MIKE ALLRED
	LAURA ALLRED
"White Hating Coon" Artwork	**JOE QUESADA**
	JIMMY PALMIOTTI

"Idiosyncratic" & "Baby Dave" Artwork	**KIRK VAN WORMER**
Assistant Costume Designer	**MELISSA CRAWFORD**
Hair / Make-Up Artist	**JANE CHOI**
Hair/ Make-Up Assistant	**KRISTIN MOSIER**
Postproduction Manager	**MONICA HAMPTON**
Assistant AVID Editor	**DAVID GLASER**
AVID Editorial at	**GIZMO ENTERPRISES, INC.**
	POST PERFECT, INC.
Supervising Sound Editor	**BRIAN MACKEWICH**
Sound Designers	**BRIAN MACKEWICH**
	DAVID GLASER
Sound Editors	**DAVID GLASER**
	SEAN McAULIFFE
Postproduction Sound Editing at	**BAM MEDIA SERVICES, INC.**
Foley Artists	**GARY FUNICELLI**
	DAVID GLASER
	DON HANKINSON
	BRIAN MACKEWICH
	SUSAN MACKEWICH
	SEAN McAULIFFE
	DON POWELL
Supervising ADR Editor	**BRIAN MACKEWICH**
Music Editing	**BRIAN MACKEWICH**
	DAVID GLASER
	SEAN McAULIFFE
Rerecording Mixer	**DOMINICK "THE DOMINATOR" TAVELLA**
Negative Cutter	**NOËLLE PENRAAT**
Color Timer	**FRED HEID**
Titles & Opticals	**REI MEDIA GROUP, N.Y.**
Production Sound Mixer	**WILLIAM KOZY**
Boom Operator	**JOSEPH WHITE, JR.**

Assistant Production Coordinator	**BRYAN JOHNSON**
Script Supervisor	**PEGGY SUTTON**
Gaffer	**LEARAN "SKIPPY" KAHANOV**
Best Boy Electric	**ALAN JACOBSEN**
Third Electric	**TAKESHI HATTORI**
Additional Electrics	**ANDREW BLAUNER**
	ERIC BONCHER
	RAFAEL GOSSE-GARDET
	KEVIN HACKENBERG
	ELIZABETH WICK
Rigging Electric	**JEREMY GRAHAM**
Key Grip	**PETER VIETRO-HANNUM**
Grip Best Boy and Ice Dolly Grip	**MICHAEL "RODI" RODIA**
Third Grip	**SETH LOFT**
Additional Grips	**DIVINE COX**
	JOHN McENERNEY
	M.C. MURRAY
	CHRISTIAN O'REILLY
Rigging Grip	**ROBERTO LOPEZ**
	NAT RUSSELL
Firearms Specialist	**DAVID McCOLE**
2nd Second Assistant Director	**CHIP SIGNORE**
Key Set PA	**GLENN MOBLEY**
Set PA's	**NICK GIOVANNETTI**
	SHAI HALPERIN
	MIKE HANSEN
	VINCENT PEREIRA
	DEVON J. START
	KYLE V. WHITE
	MIKE ZITTEL
	NICOLE DURYEA
	DAVID HURLBURT
	JAY CHANDRASEKHAR

Key Office PA	**GARY VANDER-VOORT**
Office PA's	**CHRISTOPHER CRAM**
	RANDI EATON
	DOUG EDWARDS
	CARLO HART
	AMANDA NANAWA
Art Department PA's	**JOHN CARLUCCI**
	AMANDA NANAWA
Location Assistants	**DAVID RHEE**
	KAREN PHILLIPS
Construction Coordinator	**MIKE "GOLD BOND" BAKER**
Construction Foreman	**SCOTT "WHITEY" ANDERSON**
Scenic Artists	**KATE BARTOLDUS**
	MITCHELL LANDSMAN
Publicist	**WEISSMAN / ANGELOTTI**
Casting Director	**SHANA LORY**
Extras Casting	**PARIS PETRICK**
Key Craft Service	**BRIAN LYNCH**
Craft Service Assistant	**BRYAN W. STRANG**
Caterers	**THE BROADWAY GRILL**
Catered by	**JOHN T. COPELAND**
	RITAMARIE STAPLETON
	COLLEEN LYNCH

Insurance provided by
GREAT NORTHERN / REIFF & ASSOC.

Legal Services provided by
SLOSS LAW OFFICE / JOHN SLOSS
/ JODI PEIKOFF / PAUL BRENNAN

Banking Services provided by
REPUBLIC NATIONAL BANK OF NEW YORK

Film Processing provided by
GUFFANTI FILM LABORATORIES, INC.

The director would like to thank

GOD
For all that's come before, all that'll come after,
and most importantly, for right now.

JOEY
For giving me something personal to say. I love you, poopie.
(First one who laughs gets decked!)

SCOTT
Master of the Impossible, ying to my yang, heart of my heart . . .
He's my cherry pie.

BEN
Outstanding. Outstanding, this guy.

JASON LEE
For kicking it Reynold's style.

DWIGHT
Hi Duh-Wight.

JAY
My little Mewes.

JON GORDON
Why, Why, Why?!?

MOM & DAD
I know I've got a PG in me somewhere.

JOHN PIERSON

Guru, Czar, friend.

DAVE

For the prettiest pictures yet.

At bargain basement prices, no less!

BOB HAWK

For being there from the start,

teaching us what makes a movie great,

and always doing the dishes.

HARVEY

Who, like a good parent, gives us money,

offers endless moral support,

and spanks us when we need spanking

(okay . . . everything but the spanking part).

MIKE ALLRED

For fulfilling this fanboy's dream. See you in the funny papers.

THE CAST AND CREW

Who worked for nothing, yet gave everything.

MATT SEITZ

For the one review that made a difference.

BRIAN MACKEWICH AND BAM

For the extra mile . . . and the hundred more that followed.

And to the critics who hated our last flick—all is forgiven.

Filmed with ARRIFLEX Camera & Lenses

provided by OPPENHEIMER CAMERA

When in Red Bank visit JAY & SILENT BOB'S SECRET STASH—
Comics, Games & Cool Swag.

Come see the View Askewniverse
at http://www.viewaskew.com

JAY AND SILENT BOB WILL RETURN IN "DOGMA" . . . (promise)